# CULLODEN TALES

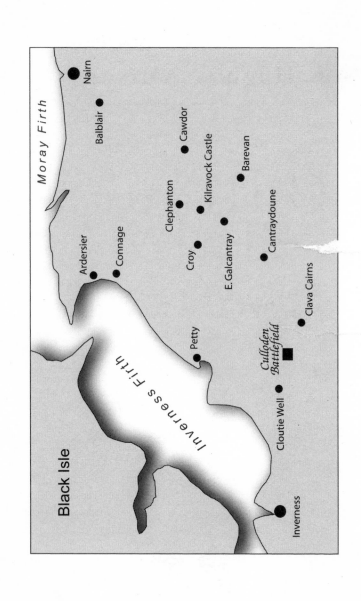

Hugh G. Allison

# Culloden Tales

## Stories From Scotland's
## Most Famous Battlefield

MAINSTREAM
PUBLISHING

EDINBURGH AND LONDON

Reprinted 2008

First published in Great Britain in 2007 by
MAINSTREAM PUBLISHING COMPANY
(EDINBURGH) LTD
7 Albany Street
Edinburgh EH1 3UG

ISBN 9781845962395

A catalogue record for this book is available
from the British Library

Typeset in Bembo

Printed in Great Britain by
CPI William Clowes Ltd, Beccles, NR34 7TL

For Dawn,
whose support is my strength
and whose belief has brought this
collection to life

# Acknowledgements

Over a quarter of a million people visit Culloden every year. Of those, a reasonable proportion also choose to pass the time of day at the front desk. I would like to thank them for their interest, their stories and also their questions. It is often the enquiries of others that spark new trains of thought in ourselves, and set us off and running to research some innovative or different approach.

The idea for *Culloden Tales* had its genesis in just such an exchange. One Mrs MacGregor, visiting the battlefield in February 2006, told me a wonderful story (included at the beginning of Part Three). When I complimented her on the holding of such a tale, she suggested to me that I was working in just the right place to record this kind of story from the visitors. So thank you, Mrs MacGregor, wherever you may be. This book could be described as the fruit of our conversation.

And the rest, as they say, is history.

Thanks, then, are due to all of those people who carried their stories safely to Culloden and then agreed for those same stories to appear in the pages of this book.

I would also like to single out for special thanks my patient and long-suffering friends and relatives, who have brought improvement to the finished work by repeated readings of the raw text, followed by suggestions and support. This time around these include David K.M. Allison, Dawn Allison, Kerry Allison, Lindsay Allison, Howard Cockburn, Duncan Cook, Carol MacDonald, Deirdre Smyth and George Stevenson.

Thanks to Katy Jordan of *Source* magazine; William Forbes for the Clach an Airm piece; and Greg Dawson Allen and Howard Anstruther. And to Andrew Duke, whose photographs throughout the book add so much atmosphere. Alan Bain, of the American–Scottish Foundation, and (Miss) Duncan MacDonald, of the Caledonian Foundation, both believed in and supported this book. Thank you.

In the course of writing *Culloden Tales*, I have had to rely upon help, information and advice from a large range of sources. These include the National Library, the National Archive of Scotland, the National Museums of Scotland and the National Trust for Scotland Library. Regional and local organisations have also been of assistance, including the Gaelic Society of Inverness and the West Highland Museum.

Individual researcher Peter Gallagher was invaluable at the National Archives at Kew and Debra Barrie, managing editor of the journal *Proceedings of the Society of Antiquaries of Scotland*, made it easy to include the map of the Galcantray excavations. Being able to access such a wealth of historical sources has kept me encouraged and enthusiastic.

I owe very specific gratitude to the authors of those works from which I have taken short quotes to help me clarify portions of the narrative: George Bruce and Paul H. Scott (eds.) *A Scottish Postbag*; Peter Anderson, *Culloden Moor and the Story of the Battle*; and Sandy MacLennan, *Source* magazine, 1st series, issue 7, 1987.

The National Trust for Scotland is the modern–day steward of the battlefield and is to be commended for its management and care of the site. I would like to thank the staff for practical help and encouragement and for access to the considerable library of Jacobite literature available on site.

My former colleagues at the Highland Council have been supportive in many ways. Thanks are due in particular to Andrew Ferguson in Nairn, staff at the Nairn library and those in both the Genealogy Unit and the reference room at Inverness library who helped with the project. I have also been assisted and encouraged by historians, such as Professor Christopher Duffy; archaeologists, such as Dr Tony Pollard; members of the 1745 Association, such as Sonia Cameron Jacks; and many uncounted others.

Finally, it is great to be working with Mainstream Publishing again, as they make turning a disk into a book a wholly magical experience. Thank you all.

# Contents

# Introduction

This book is a new look at an old event. The Battle of Culloden has been extensively researched and is the focus of many different works, both popular and scholarly. However, this book takes a genuinely fresh and innovative view of the subject and attempts to answer the real questions that visitors ask.

As a site of heritage pilgrimage, Culloden attracts people from across the world. These people, when they come, often bring with them the most outstanding stories, which have been held safe by their family down through the generations.

The battlefield is a poignant location, resonant with past deeds and emotive memories, and those who work the place are rarely unaffected. Their stories, recorded here too, carry weight and add to the undeniable reputation of the field.

I write this introduction 200 years to the day since Sir Walter Scott wrote a letter to a friend (as can be seen in Bruce and Scott's anthology, *A Scottish Postbag*), in which he said of an old Jacobite, Stewart of Invernahyle:

> I believe there never was a man who united the ardour
> of a soldier and tale-teller – a man of talk as they call
> it in Gaelic – in such an excellent degree, and he was
> as fond of telling as I was of hearing. I became a valiant
> Jacobite at the age of 10 years . . . Certainly I will not

renounce the idea of doing something to preserve these
stories, and the memory of times and manners which,
though existing as it were yesterday, have so strangely
vanished from our eyes. Whether this will be best done
by collecting the old tales, or by modernising them
as subjects of legendary poetry, I have never seriously
considered, but your kind encouragement confirms me
in the resolution that something I must do, and that
speedily . . .

As long as people come to see the battlefield, they will bring tales
and, as Sir Walter Scott saw those two centuries ago, it is a service,
perhaps even a duty, to record these tales for the future. I work front-
of-house at the visitor centre and so it seems to be up to me now to
do my part, collecting stories and setting them down here. Dozens
of exciting new accounts have been gathered and are offered as a
unique record of the power of the location and its status as a place
of pilgrimage to which returning exiles bring their history.

The book is presented in four distinct parts. This is to provide the
reader with structure, and so avoid the danger of simply producing
a welter of anecdotes.

Part One is entitled 'Tales from the Past'. These stories are
gathered from the local area from the time frame pre-dating the
battle. There are descriptions of the earliest times and peoples. The
astronomy and ritual of the mysterious Clava Cairns is explored
and the Cloutie Well is visited in the same context – that of ancient
Celtic belief and religion.

Time then moves forward, and in quick succession follow a
clutch of tales telling of the coming of the Romans, the arrival of
Christianity and the life and times of the Dark Age Celts who were
the ancestors of those who fought and fell at Culloden.

Callum Beg, the poacher, is the subject of a brace of more
modern anecdotes, outlining some of his outrageous feats in the
hills around Strathnairn and Streens.

Part One culminates with a look at the phenomenon of second sight, and the man known as the Brahan Seer. His two prophecies, made in the century before the battle, describe it eerily well.

Part Two is called 'Tales from the Battle'. It begins with a history of the Stewart dynasty in Scotland, up to and including the Union of the Crowns of both Scotland and England in 1603. The backgrounds to the Jacobite risings are then examined, including the '45 up to the moments before the Battle of Culloden commences.

Then, one by one, we hear of the parts played – before, during and, in some cases, after the battle – by at least 14 of the principal clan regiments involved. There were probably more non-Highlanders than Highlanders involved in the Jacobite army and we hear about some of their regiments too.

The full tragedy and weight of the aftermath to Culloden fell upon the Highlands however, and that is why the clan regiments are focused on. These are their stories.

Part Two concludes with battle and aftermath scenes, a look at some particularly intriguing what-ifs and a consideration of Culloden today, as an international icon.

Part Three, 'Tales by Way of the Door', is a collection of tales chosen from the array brought to us at the visitor centre by people from all corners of the globe – Scotland, England, Canada, Sweden, Australia, New Zealand, the USA and Belgium.

The story that stimulated my original concept for this book is here, featuring strong drink, a jailbreak, a baby and the emigrant ship, *Hector*. Other tales include artefacts and treasure handed from father to son, heroes such as Major Gillies MacBean, and remembrances of what happened to some of the prisoners – and indeed some of the escapees.

Taken together, these tales represent the precious cargo that emigrants take with them, and often protect and preserve better than those who remain. In these cases, distance from home seems to increase value.

Part Four is simply 'Tales from Those who Work on the Moor'. The stories here belong to tour guides, battlefield staff and local people, and range from the supernatural, such as 'The Skree of Culloden', through to the inexplicable, like the relationship that local postie Susannah from Germany has with the site. There are family secrets and inheritances, and tales of coincidence, like the connection between a staff member and the Duke of Tarentum, and the relationship of the Duke, in turn, to Bonnie Prince Charlie.

Part Four rounds off with 'The Archaeologist's Tale', which includes the most up-to-date discoveries, finds and ongoing searches being made on the field.

Throughout the book, I have tried to follow a couple of simple rules in order to better inform the reader. Wherever possible, when the text is describing specific historical episodes and actions, I have used what is known as the three-source rule. This requires that three independent sources be found describing a specific incident before giving it credence as having happened. This should assure the reader and give them confidence in the facts they are reading.

When I have neither primary data from the time nor three independent sources, I use a form of words such as 'It is sometimes said . . .' When relating stories told by a third party, my job is to ensure that I pass on the tale accurately, as told to me. The content of the tale is a matter for its owner.

So read on. These Culloden Tales have been gathered for you.

# Prologue

On then, into action;
And as you go, think of those that went before you
and of those that shall come after.

These words are a clarion call to battle, and it is easy to
think of them as an entreaty to the Jacobites standing on
Drummossie ridge – a whaleback, rising some 600 feet above the
coastal plain east of Inverness.

The Battle of Culloden, raging across the high points of this
ridge in 1746, has inspired tales the world over. However time did
not start, and stop, on 16 April 1746. That was only one day in a
series of days. Drummossie Moor has been a landmark for many
peoples, for many millennia.

The call to action quoted above was not Jacobite. In fact, it was
uttered almost two millennia earlier, by Calgacus, leader of the
Caledonians, as he faced the Romans somewhere in the north-east
of Scotland. He understood the power that rested in the idea of
people as one link in the chain that is history.

There is more than one potent concept crafted boldly within
his words. They suggest the depth of old traditions and the roots of
the people in the land. They also serve to remind us of the richness
and validity of *all* of the stories and tales from the area around

Drummossie. In particular, they remind us of the history from earliest times, which is sometimes hard to see, back through the all-obscuring cannon smoke of the final Jacobite defeat in 1746.

The stories which follow, in particular in Part One, are included here to help give a broader understanding of the local area and the local people – and a wider look, too, at the range of stories which we can call *Culloden Tales*.

# PART ONE

# TALES FROM THE PAST

**Before Mons Graupius**

Which will you choose – to follow your leader into battle, or submit to all the tribulations of slavery?

Whether you are to endure these for ever or take quick vengeance, this field must decide.

On then, into action;

And as you go, think of those that went before you and of those that shall come after.

– Calgacus

# Register of Tales

## Tabula Rasa

The air was warm and a breeze guttered fitfully across the surface of the vast sea, Lake Orcadie. The earth's first forests fringed the shore and huge rivers wound downhill, dropping enormous loads of sediment eroded from the ranges of earlier Caledonian mountains. This was the Devonian period (about 400 million years ago) and our area was south of the equator but moving steadily north. These deposits became the rocks known as Middle Old Red Sandstone and find local exposure as the Leanach sandstones, and the Nairnside and Clava shales and flagstones.

By the time the Ice Age arrived, it was practically modern times – a mere 12,000 years ago. Whatever flora and fauna had flourished immediately before the Ice Age was now a thing of the past. The animals would have fled before the advancing ice. The vegetation would have been crushed under it. With ice a mile thick in places, the whole country was being scraped clear beneath it. When the ice melted, by around 8000 BC, the landscapes revealed were blasted and desolate – a glaciated wasteland of gravel terraces, boulder beds and gouged valleys.

The scoured Drummossie ridge, littered with glacial boulders, seemed to loom above. This may have been partly due to the Nairn valley to the south having been deepened and gravelled by the passage of ice. The area had become a *tabula rasa* – a clean slate – upon which the future could be written.

The future was slow in arriving, however. It took several hundred years for suitable soils to develop, followed by colonisation by the first hardy plants. It was probably about a thousand years after the ice that the era known as 'the Wildwood' was established. The woods in this area contained birch, hazel, oak and pine, and were home to bears, wolves and wild boar, as well as many other mammals still familiar in later times.

# Drawing Metal from Stone

During the Wildwood period, the only eyes looking at the ridge of Drummossie belonged to the beasts of the earth and the birds of the air. Eventually, the first curious people started to drift into the area. These were a nomadic people, often following the movements of either shoals of fish or game for hunting. Although they lived during the period known as the Stone Age, they were nothing like the cavemen that inhabit our imaginations. They hunted, fished and gathered shellfish, all very successfully. Their societies were defined and shaped by complex combinations of art, culture and religion. These were the Mesolithic people, who began to leave evidence of themselves here from around 5600 BC.

Then came the Neolithic period, or New Stone Age, from around 4000 BC. The big change in lifestyle at this point was the introduction of farming. People began to clear the Wildwood in earnest and to domesticate both animals and plants in order to provide themselves with a more reliable food supply. These were innovations that had developed in the Eastern Mediterranean, 2,000–3,000 years earlier and had spread throughout Continental Europe.

The first farmers in the Culloden area settled along the coastal plain and the valley of the River Nairn. The main summit of Drummossie ridge was avoided, as it was exposed to the worst of the elements, was difficult to traverse and had only poor, thin clays for soil.

Then, around 2200 BC, a marvellous discovery was made, changing the lives of these early peoples. This find was the almost magical ability to smelt copper ore at very high temperatures (1,083 degrees Celsius) and then mix the resulting shimmering molten liquid with tin to create hard, practical metal useable in the making of tools and ornaments. The Bronze Age had arrived.

# The Good Stones

The south bank of the River Nairn was sheltered from the coastal weather by Drummossie ridge and yet did not lie within the shadow of the high ground. The gravel terrace found here was a favoured location, safe from all but the worst floods, and an excellent place for the Bronze Age farming settlement that claimed it.

It was about the year 2000 BC that someone in this community was overcome by a vision of staggering significance. Discussing it excitedly with the others, the vision was refined, and reworked, until it took a form everyone could embrace. Working together, the community would clear away their settlement, which could be rebuilt elsewhere, and by using a mix of existing materials and some special stone quarried for the purpose, they would raise a ritual landscape of extraordinary design and spirituality. These inspired monuments would align with celestial events and thus mark significant anniversaries throughout the calendar.

The people went on to raise a variety of structures, including domed passage-grave cairns and a ring cairn with rays, or causeways, each cairn encompassed by an impressive stone circle. The largest standing stones on site were quarried and brought uphill from the River Nairn – a task involving at least a dozen workers.

The intervening years have drawn a veil over some aspects of this remarkable site and this stimulates a question or two. Each passage grave was in use for only a short time, and each seems to contain just one single burial. Who might these people have been? Were they perhaps prominent? Or were they chosen by some other means?

The ring cairn was never covered and may have been the site for various ceremonies, relating either to burials or to the turning of the year. What form might such ceremonies have taken? To whom, and how, did they worship? There are cup-marked stones at each of the cairns: were these stones re-used from an earlier time when, set flat, the 'cups' could contain ritual offerings for the spirits, such as milk or cheese?

These questions, among others, are likely to remain unanswered and, as such, merely add to the sense of mystery found amidst these stones. At the same time, however, some elements of this site are so bold that they seem to tell a clear story, even thousands of years later.

Balnuaran of Clava is the name of the place where these monuments stand. One translation of Clava Cairns is given as 'the good stones', which seems appropriate, given their obvious association with the cycle of the seasons and the farming year.

There is ample evidence that these cairns, like many others, were orientated on the position of the moon, particularly on events known as the minor and major lunar standstills, when the moon is at its most southern point of setting. Clava is unusual, however, in that it is also orientated on the sun. The cairns stand with their backs to the north-east, and the passage open to the south-west. They align perfectly on the midwinter solstice during which, on clear evenings, the rays of the setting sun would travel down the passage and a beam of intense light would focus on the back wall of the central chamber. The sun, as viewed from the north-east cairn at this time, would appear to set into the south-west cairn. The strong north-east/south-west axis to these cairns also indicates that the relationship with the midsummer sunrise seems to be important.

The most unique feature of the Clava Cairns is that, compared to the solid building techniques developed and used centuries earlier in the Neolithic period, the structural-engineering involved at Clava is, at the very least, eccentric. Choice of fragile building materials, lack of concern for stability and the use of graded uprights all combine to show that significant structural stability was sacrificed in favour of aesthetics, orientation and ritual design.

This was a site where the builders were determined that spirit would triumph over physical form.

So what elements were so important as to take precedence over solid stonework? There were five: orientation, colour, numbers, decoration and design.

In addition to the solar and lunar alignments at midwinter and midsummer, it has been observed that as the sun moves along the horizon throughout the year, the shadows of specific standing stones (at sunrise and sunset) will touch cup-marked stones in the cairn kerbs. These shadows show the times of spring and autumn equinox, as well as the ancient Celtic festivals of Beltane (May), Lughnasa (August), Samhain (November) and Bride (February).

All aspects of these buildings were soaked in colour when new. The stone circles and the cairns themselves were built from warm red stones on their south-western side and would have glowed in the sunset light. They were built from whiter stone, including gneiss and quartz, on their north-eastern side, which would have flashed and sparkled at the rising of the sun.

The number twelve (or multiples of it) appears in many parts of these cairns' structures, such as the number of stones in the circles, or in the outer kerbs, or in the inner kerb of the ring cairn, or of stones used in building the passage in either cairn.

The decoration provided by the cup-marked stones has been noted, appearing on some of the standing stones of the circles, as well as being incorporated in the cairns.

In design, all of the main components of the site are graded by height. The stone circles, cairn kerbs and even the central chamber foundation stones are all smaller at the back (or north-east) and rise to their tallest height to the front (or south-west). The cairns also had rubble platforms added around them, probably when the passages were closed up, and the spirits were left to dream quietly for a few centuries.

Generations passed and, unfortunately, a savage and sustained deterioration in the climate set in. The people had grown numerous during the good years. Now, crop failure was an ever more frequent occurrence and there were too many mouths to feed. What were they to do? The idea of reusing the old monuments and temples, and even building new ones, seemed to provide an answer. Perhaps with a renewal of due spiritual observance the harvests would improve.

This is one theory explaining the reuse of the passage graves for cremation and burial, and also the construction of the Kerb Cairn at Clava. Built around 1000 BC, this cairn is a cruder construct than those built 1,000 years earlier and is perhaps only about 30 feet in diameter. However, some similar features resurface, such as colour as a theme – here, pink and red boulders alternate with white. The stones may originally have bounded a low earth mound, and a cup- and ring-marked stone (probably taken from elsewhere) was set into the kerb.

None of this improved the harvest, however, and the inevitable followed. The easy days had gone. More weapons were being manufactured and settlements began to be fortified, or at the very least enclosed. Land became wealth, and force became one means of accessing it. As time and effort turned towards defence, there was a decline in the construction of any further elaborate stone circles or temples, and the people began seeing wells, trees and natural features as places of power, and also as places of observance.

The structures at Clava, raised with such vision and such effort, would now be left to fall slowly into a second sleep of centuries. Those heady days of power and colour and intensity would fade, but never be entirely forgotten. There will be some people, even thousands of years later, who will still make observance at the Good Stones.

# Tobar na H'Oige

Like the turning of the seasons, the Bronze Age passed away and the people moved restlessly forward, into the Iron Age. By about 700 BC, the profession of metalsmith began to assume an almost mystical stature. This was because iron was considerably more difficult to work than bronze; however, it was a much harder metal and therefore of more use in the creation of tools, and also weapons, in those increasingly warlike times.

Although these Iron Age Celts were farmers, they were also fierce warriors. They are likely to have spoken a language related to modern-day Welsh and locally occupied the same lands as their ancestors – the Nairn valley and the coastal plain. The men would have stood at around 5 ft 8 in. and, if they avoided a violent death in their youth, would have expected to survive to around 40 years of age. The women were around 5 ft 3 in. tall and, if long-lived, they might have reached the age of 50.

Their health was unremarkable: natural herbal remedies were used for the most common ailments, while faith, religious ceremony and magic may have been required in order to combat more serious problems. The places of power in the landscape were sought to carry out such rituals. Tobar na H'Oige, on the north slope of Drummossie ridge, was one such place.

This well has been in use as a Cloutie Well since earliest times, the water originally being considered sacred – not only because water represents Danu, the mother goddess, symbolising abundance, but also because the Salmon of Knowledge lived in such waters. Traditionally, people visit this well at Beltane, the May festival of spring and rebirth. They dip a rag, or cloutie, belonging to them into the well water. Then they tie it to a nearby tree in the belief that all their ailments and troubles will leave them and transfer to the rag until it rots away. Those who may think it a fine joke to remove a rag from the tree should be aware that those ailments stored within it would then transfer to them!

Sandy MacLennan, writing in *Source*, the Holy Wells journal, explained:

> Long ago, when I was young, there were buses run, on the first Sunday in May, to the Cloutie Well, four miles from Inverness, so that the throngs might make their devotions. A silver coin in the well, a sip of the water, three circuits deiseal [sunwise, or clockwise] and a shred of clothing on one of the nearby trees and the rite was done.

> It was an ancient ritual. Of that there was no doubt, though few participating knew how old, and its meaning was lost in the distant past, long before we were seduced and bound by tales from the Middle East. We, who had defied the legions for four centuries, succumbing to the new emissaries of Rome. But that's another story. The centuries have passed. An alternative version from dissidents in Geneva has bound us again, but still the ritual at the well persists, still around the wells scattered through what once were Celtic realms, the rags flutter on the trees.

The well was later to become known as St Mary's Well. This was an attempt by the Church, in the sixteenth century, to replace earlier pagan ritual with at least a semblance of Christianity, by using such sites as holy wells.

The well is located in Culloden Woods, within the original lands of Culloden House. Indeed, it is said that it was one of the Forbes of Culloden who built an encircling wall and had paving put down because his wife went there to bathe; and it was another Forbes who required a bridge over the railway to carry the footpath leading to the well.

Although the well is most often used as a wishing well nowadays, there is no doubting that these sacred waters have a continuous story as a place of pilgrimage.

# Agricola's Seventh Campaign

Rome invaded during the Iron Age. Julius Agricola became governor of Britain in AD 78. The Flavian dynasty controlled the Roman Empire at that time, which is why Agricola's seven offensives are often called the Flavian campaigns.

It was Agricola's seventh campaign, in AD 84, which brought him to the neighbourhood of the Moray Firth. A chain of large marching camps charted his progress up the east coast and through Aberdeenshire, towards the River Spey. The native inhabitants are said to have amassed an army more than 30,000 strong under the legendary warrior Calgacus.

That army was soundly defeated by Agricola at the Battle of Mons Graupius – a possible mistranslation of 'Grampian Mountains'. This left Agricola unopposed in the Moray Firth area and with a desire to consolidate his gains, by sea and by land.

At sea, he deployed his fleet along the southern shore of the Moray Firth. They passed the mouth of the River Lossie, calling it Ostium Loxa Fluvius, and entered the Beauly Firth, looking for a through channel, naming it Varar. They also named the people who lived on the shores of the Inner Moray Firth, calling them the Vacomagi, meaning 'the border people'.

Even if not a border region, there is ample evidence that this area had already been a place of meeting, or cross-fertilisation, for thousands of years: a place where many quite different cultural traditions have come into contact.

On land, as suggested by the late Professor G.D.B. Jones, Agricola would have wished to construct a string of Flavian forts in the vicinity. Working on this likelihood, Professor Jones initiated a programme of fieldwork and aerial surveys in the 1980s. In 1984, at Easter Galcantray, just four miles east of Culloden, an aerial survey identified crop markings on the south bank of the Nairn, suggesting the presence of a rectangular ditched enclosure. Floods and river erosion had taken the northern half of the enclosure, however. The remaining portion had a centrally placed entrance on its southern side and exhibited traits generally typical of a small Flavian fort, in both size and design.

Professor Jones spent the next six years excavating this feature and gathering further evidence. Unflustered by contrary opinions raised by other Romanists, he set out the results of his six seasons of painstaking excavations. They include evidence of a six-post timber gateway, four rectangular timber buildings the same size and form as the usual Roman barrack blocks, an eight-post timber angle-tower in the south-west corner and a line of post-pits for timber bracing holding the enclosure rampart.

These findings are best illustrated by the inclusion of the plan from Richard A. Gregory's paper, 'Excavations along the Moray Firth Littoral', published in *Proceedings of the Society of Antiquaries of Scotland* (volume 131, 2001).

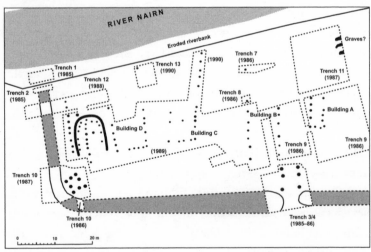

*The location of excavation trenches at Easter Galcantray*
*(With kind permission,* Proceedings of the Society of
Antiquaries of Scotland*)*

The ditches are V-shaped and show signs of having been re-cut – but only once. Re-cutting ditches was generally undertaken every year, so a story unfolds of a structure which was only occupied for a couple of years.

In addition, the ditches were thereafter deliberately back-filled with rampart material and building debris, and the site levelled. The radiocarbon date for this is around the end of the first century. This would fit perfectly with the hasty abandonment of the northern holdings, when the Legion II Adiutrix was pulled out of Britain due to the Danube crisis around AD 86.

All of Professor Jones's findings suggested to him that he was working within the remains of a single-period timber-built fort of around 550 feet square in extent. In size, it resembles a small infantry fort, like that of Fendoch, at the mouth of the Sma' Glen, near Crieff.

After its rapid abandonment, the site was reclaimed by nature. Grass grew and both the years and the generations passed. The two years of occupation was nothing measured against this, yet it is certainly long enough for bored legionaries to look for local entertainment and diversion. It is, therefore, a perfectly reasonable supposition that there may be more than a little evidence of Roman visitation still visible within the area, if one were to look carefully!

## The Dove and the King

From Culloden, the Great Glen opens to the south-west. This is one of the great routeways that make this area such a crossroads. New ideas had been travelling up the route since before Clava Cairns were built.

The time is now AD 565 and another new idea is making its way up the glen. The man bringing it is St Columba – Colm Cille, or Dove of the Church. He is travelling to the court of Bridei, or Brude, son of Maelchon, King of the Picts, and is bringing the

Christian message. The tale of this meeting is well known but not straightforward. Questions arise regarding issues of belief, location and outcomes . . . and these all occur in threes.

Early accounts of Columba's life don't state that he converted King Bridei, merely that the Pictish King held Columba in high honour and that they were soul friends. The Druids continued to exercise all their old influence over the King, so it is not known: (1) whether Bridei ever converted to Christianity; (2) whether he was already a Christian; or (3) whether Columba converted him.

With regard to where Bridei held court, again there are three possibilities. St Columba's biographer, Adamnan, wrote that the court was atop a steep rock and that after leaving the Royal court, Columba soon afterwards came to the River Ness. These observations have led to thoughts that the court must, most likely, have been located at: (1) Craig Phadrig; (2) Torvean; or (3) the current Castle Hill.

Scholars have spent centuries debating these choices, but for us what is important are the results of the meeting between these two men, a Scot and a Pict, in the shadow of Drummossie. As this was a political as well as a religious mission, it: (1) built the bridge between the peoples, making us Scots, and not Picts, today; (2) ushered in the art and learning that the Celtic Church encouraged; and (3) brought the religion that, over 1,000 years later, would pitch the monarchy into the Jacobite crisis.

## Clann

At the time of Columba's visit to Bridei, society in the Highlands could be described as tribal. From that time onwards, and as the Scots kingdom of Dalriada gained prominence, a new word began cropping up in Highland documents and sources: clan.

'*Clann*' is a Gaelic word, which translates as 'children'. A clan, therefore, would be an extended family group, sometimes descendants of a common ancestor. Kinship, then, was seen as a principal factor in defining a clan, though location also had a part to play. As a term derived from Scots Gaelic, it is easy to make the association that the clans were, in general, those people living in the Gaelic-speaking area to the north of the Highland Line.

The Highland Line was not just a notation on a map, it was a physical barrier: a fault line running south-west to north-east, from Helensburgh on the west coast to Stonehaven on the east. Travellers could feel the point of crossover, the passing from one land into the other. Bankfoot, north of Perth, for example, is well named, as it sits just on the downslope of the Highland Line.

These concepts of kinship and geography, although generalisations, help explain the Gaelic way of asking where someone is from: 'Cò às a tha sibh?' translating as 'Who are you from?' This also goes some way to answering the question 'What is a clan?'

Kinship was what bound the leading families of any clan together but, in a social system based on territorial expansion, numbers of men could be critical. Sometimes, when a clan was acquiring land quickly, it outgrew its own ability to populate the new clanlands. One solution was to forcibly assimilate and rename the original population. Another option was to attract new clansmen by offering a sack of meal, or even a portion of land, to anyone willing to take the clan name – hence the arising of the term 'mealie clansmen'.

There were as many exceptions to the rule of geography as there were to that of kinship. Clans in different parts of the Highlands developed from Norse, Pictish, Scottish, Anglian and Norman stock, depending upon their location. Travel to the extreme northeast would bring the traveller back out of the Highlands altogether and into the deeply ingrained Norse culture of the Caithness area.

An oft-repeated question at Culloden today is 'Where did the clans come from, and how old are they?' Many clans vie to be recognised as amongst the oldest in the Highlands. But which of them belong among that group is a question guaranteed to get a spirited argument going, even to this day. Some people say that Clan MacAlpin, for example, descend from Kenneth MacAlpin, the first king of the united peoples of the Picts and Scots in AD 843. Clan MacNeil claim descent from the Irish High King Niall of the Nine Hostages, who lived in the first half of the fifth century. Clan Robertson (Clann Donnachaidh) claim descent from King Duncan I, who reigned from 1034. Clan Ferguson say that they descend from Fergus I, King of Scots, AD 500.

Then there are the younger clans. As clans grew, they often subdivided, and so cadet families would branch from the main stem. These often took the name of the person who first led them. Thus the MacAlisters are the earliest Cadet Family of the MacDonalds, and their founder was Alasdair MacDonnell, younger brother to Angus Mor, chief of Clan Donald, circa 1262–1300.

The lands controlled by any given clan varied throughout the centuries, as the power of the clans waxed and waned. Watching change in clan territory, over time, was sometimes like watching tides, running to full and then running out again. Some clans amassed huge power and extensive clanlands, while others became completely extinct, their name now only a footnote in history. The one thing that was certain was . . . that nothing was certain. This was a dynamic system, fuelled by both political intrigue and raw strength.

The clans in the vicinity of Drummossie had a variety of illustrious ancestors. As we have heard, the Bronze Age peoples were the engineers responsible for building the Good Stones in the valley of the River Nairn. Their descendants, strengthened by waves of Pictish immigrants, were later dubbed the Vacomagi by the Romans, who may themselves have widened the gene pool. Together they went on to become a nation ruled by Bridei, from his stronghold in Inverness. The Great Glen continued to provide a strategic routeway across the

Highlands, and Inverness developed at its north-eastern extreme. This was the crucial bridging and fording point near the mouth of the River Ness. Both the land and the people have therefore contributed to the settlement long being known as the capital of the Highlands. A case for kinship and geography again.

The clan system became well established throughout the Middle Ages, AD 1100 onwards. As the society developed and clans began to include subdivided branches (known as septs or cadet families), the chief of the strongest branch might become known as a captain of a confederacy.

Inheritance of chiefship was not always by the eldest legitimate son. The system of tanistry was practised, which meant that the leading families could, if necessary, choose the next chief from the able-bodied and high born among their number. He would be known as the tanist choice. To complicate things further, in the Highlands 'handfasting' was a form of trial marriage, which lasted for a year and a day. If it proved unfruitful, it could be terminated at the end of that time, but sometimes a chief might die or be slain before his handfast union could be regularised and, in this case, his son was still recognised as a potential successor.

As an acknowledgment of his authority, all the clansmen paid tribute to the chief, often in the form of a bond of manrent for offence and defence.

There had been no reason for the clan system to move far from its tribal roots . . . until the coming of the Normans. The first hint of things to come would be seen in the eleventh century, with the disruptions brought by Malcolm II, as he tried to clear the way to the throne for his grandson, Duncan. It was Duncan's grandson, David I, who embarked upon an active programme of Normanisation, including land grants to new noble families and the introduction of landowning, and landholding, based upon continental feudal method.

The main difference between the clan system and the feudal system with which it was slowly replaced was that the authority of the clan chief was based on personal and blood ties, while that of the feudal superior was based upon tenure of land.

There was a certain benign paternalism and a social cooperative structure to the clan system. These, along with concepts of stewardship and sustainability for future generations, were characteristics shared by many other societies. So the word 'clan' passed into the English language, being used to describes similar societies elsewhere, such as medieval factions in Japan, or groupings within the Native American nations. These societies became casualties, first of European feudalism and later of the modern economic theories of the eighteenth century, such as Adam Smith's definitions of political economy and the mercantile system.

In response, the clan societies became conservative, valuing honour and tradition above all things. This could be seen as a bad survival mechanism, because inflexible pride often prompted tragic confrontation with the 'modern' world. Conversely, it might be seen as good, because the oral traditions kept the clans' tales alive on stormy nights when all else seemed lost. At those times, the tale-tellers would gesture to the group, saying, 'Draw closer, draw closer, come hear the tales of the clans.'

## The Divine Right of Kings

Tanistry was not confined to the clans. Early kingship in Scotland was also determined by it. A tanist, or successor to the king, was named from among a specific group of relatives. Chosen while the current monarch still reigned, he was usually a nephew or cousin, and chosen on the basis of ability, age and health.

One other rule of tanistry seems to indicate that kingship alternated between the two main stems of the Royal house. There was also a geographical tension in the succession, as one of these branches came to draw its power from Moray (which at the time included Inverness) and the other from Atholl.

The main characteristic of tanistry, however, was that it was elective. The ruling nobles were able to choose between candidates as to who would be the next monarch. It was not until the days of Malcolm II that the Norman concept of primogeniture (dynastic succession by the firstborn son) took root. Malcolm had no sons, but one of his daughters, Bethoc, had married Crinan, Archpriest of St Columba and Abbot of Dunkeld. Malcolm, with disregard for the tanist tradition, had named their son, Duncan, as his successor.

In an effort to smooth the way for his grandson, Malcolm then began a ruthless campaign to eradicate all possible competition. He killed most of the grandchildren of Kenneth III, as they were the tanist choice, until only two remained. One of these was the Princess Gruoch, who was married to Gillecomgan, a prince (or Mormaer) of the House of Moray. They are said to have lived in a hall-house somewhere in the vicinity of Inverness (possibly to the east of the current town). This was where, in 1032, Malcolm brought his army to carry out a lightning raid on the hall-house itself. The occupants were kept inside and it was set alight, burning Gillecomgan and 50 of his followers to death.

Malcolm's raid was not entirely successful, though. Gruoch escaped, along with her infant son, Lulach, and she subsequently married Macbeth, bolstering his claim to the Scottish throne – a claim which was already stronger than Duncan's.

However, Malcolm's will prevailed and Duncan succeeded to the throne. Being also the son and hereditary heir of the archpriest Crinan, it could be argued that Duncan became Scotland's first Priest King. This view of the king as both the secular and religious leader became one of the central tenets of Scots culture thereafter.

Duncan did not rule wisely, however, and continued his grandfather's persecution of the House of Moray, along with all other potential rivals for the throne. It was while he was carrying out this policy that he was slain in battle, near Inverness, by Macbeth. It may be that King Duncan's Well, at Culcabock, in Inverness, is named for some occurrence dating from this time. Macbeth then ruled – well and wisely, we are told – for the next 17 years.

Duncan's son, Malcolm Canmore, eventually returned to Scotland from exile, and attacked and killed Macbeth in 1057. He went on to rule as Malcolm III and reinforced the concepts of dynastic succession and the divine right of kings, ensuring that both were to become part of the tradition surrounding kingship.

Although this system was not native to Scotland, and perhaps more like the style of the earlier Merovingian kings of France, it would become entrenched over the centuries and was undoubtedly a contributing factor in the intransigence of some of the later Stuart monarchs and their unshakable belief in their God–given right to rule.

There is a certain irony in the fact that the final confrontation between two sets of Malcolm II's descendants was to occur on Culloden Moor, almost in the shadow of that hall-house which he, himself, had burned to secure the succession over 700 years earlier.

## Dispossessed

Less than three miles downstream from Drummossie, on the south bank of the River Nairn, stands Cantraydoune. Nowadays it looks like nothing more than a green hillock; however, in its heyday it was a startling and impressive symbol of the feudal revolution. Cantraydoune was a Norman motte – an artificial mound of earth and clay, some 50 feet high, and surmounted by a medieval timber castle. Although no traces of the timber keep remain atop the mound, just one look at the five such strongholds woven into the Bayeux Tapestry is enough to convince anyone that it would have dominated the valley. The motte dates from around 1200, but there is no record of who raised it. It could have been any of the Norman and Flemish families who were being encouraged by the Royal House of Canmore to settle in the Highlands.

Thus Inverness was a frontier of cultural change, and the inhabitants were to be the 'the Border People' again. Malcolm Canmore's son, David I, began the Normanisation of the Highlands on coming to the throne in 1124. His grandsons, Malcolm and William 'the Lion', continued the process right into the thirteenth century.

Freskinus, a Fleming, was granted vast territories in the north and settled at Duffus, near Elgin, taking the name de Moravia (of Moray). These Morays were also later given the lordship of Petty. The Norman de Roses appeared at Geddes in Nairnshire in 1230, and in 1293 this Rose family secured Kilravock Castle by marriage. Rose of Geddes's neighbour was Sir Gervaise de Raite, another Norman, from a family called Cuming, who had been given Rait Castle. The Ogilvies were of similar heritage and were given lands close by in Strathnairn.

William the Lion issued a charter, around 1180, requiring Inverness to be fortified due to its status as a Royal outpost. Another of his charters mentions 'Geoffrey Blund, our burgess of Inverness'. This name, together with evidence of settlement pattern and early documentation, lends strength to the theory that many Flemish traders and shipwrights had been encouraged to settle in Inverness. Earl Hugh de Chatillon, the Count of St Pol, commissioned a ship to be built at Inverness in 1249 to take him and his men to the Crusades – not an order which would have been placed lightly, so he must have been confident that there were enough Flemish shipwrights available to ensure delivery.

Some changes were obvious, such as the timber Norman mansions, the planting of orchards and gardens, and the fortifying of towns, such as Inverness. Other changes were more subtle, but just as significant. The clan system began its slow journey towards feudalism. Some clan chiefs saw personal advantage in primogeniture, as it ensured that the chiefship would remain within their own immediate family. Feudalism also led to the establishment of individual ownership of land, rather than the system where land was controlled by the people who inhabited it for the benefit of the future community. This, too, was an attractive change for any chiefs who valued the contents of their purse above the people to whom they were father and leader.

The final consideration, with regards to this time of upheaval, is that these lands which were being so generously gifted to the various incoming families were not empty lands; existing clans were ousted at the coming of the Normans. Not even the strongest local clan was unaffected. The Mackintoshes found themselves dispossessed of many of their traditional estates: Petty and Daviot, given to the Morays; Strathnairn to the Ogilvies; Rait to the Cumings. All were Mackintosh lands, the loss of which would be felt down the centuries by a clan determined to regain what it saw as its rightful heritage.

It is likely that the idea of the great Clan Chattan confederation began here – a bond of mutual defence to prevent such incursions or losses to the clanlands in the future.

## The Clan of the Cat

The Clan of the Cat is the confederation of the many tribes, or clans, which could be considered local to Drummossie Moor and that part of the Highlands. In large part, their ancestors are the Vacomagi. Their tale begins with Gillichattan Mor (meaning 'Servant of St Chattan'). This man was the temporal leader of the Abbey lands of Ardchattan on Loch Etive. His extended family, and all of their descendants, became known as Clan Chattan (pronounced 'Hattan').

One of his twelfth-century descendants, Muireach Cattanach, became parson at Kingussie, and both the MacPhersons ('son of the parson') and the Davidsons – and indeed probably the MacPhails –

descend from him. The main stem of the family, however, settled in Lochaber, in Glen Loy and on Loch Arkaig-side, and their chief's seat was the stronghold of Torcastle. By the late thirteenth century, their chief was Gilpatric (also known as Dougal Dall, or Blind Dougal), sixth in line from Gillichattan Mor.

During the same period, over on the east coast, a man called Shaw (son of Duncan, third Earl of Fife) came north to assist Malcolm IV in quelling a revolt in Moray. As a reward, he was given the lands of Petty and Strathdearn and was appointed Keeper of the Royal Castle in Inverness. These grants were made about 1163. His descendants became known as Mac-an-Toiseach, or Mackintosh ('son of the leader'). The MacGillivrays joined with the Mackintoshes around 1268.

Angus, the sixth Mackintosh chief, lived at the same time as Gilpatric of Clan Chattan and married his daughter, Eva, in 1291. Marriage to Eva meant that Angus inherited the chieftainship of all of the Clan Chattan families and the lands in Lochaber. Angus and Eva lived first at Torcastle but later moved back to Rothiemurchus, in Badenoch. They were followed there by all of the adherent families of Clan Chattan.

Angus supported Robert the Bruce throughout the Wars of Independence and was rewarded with land grants as a result. Connage, by Ardersier, became the clan seat at this time and it was there that William MacBean and his four sons came, for sanctuary, shortly after – they had killed the Red Comyn's captain of Inverlochy Castle in Lochaber. Knowing that there was no love lost between Mackintosh and Comyn (Cuming) since the loss of Rait Castle to Comyn a century earlier, they put themselves under the protection of the Mackintoshes thereafter.

As Clan Chattan moved north-eastwards, their holdings in Lochaber were left empty behind them. The Camerons expanded into them, from their early territories on Locheilside. This caused inevitable tensions, ultimately resulting in armed clash and battle. Feelings grew so bitter that King Robert III had to intervene, in 1396, and propose a solution. It was decided that 30 champions from each side would fight each other to the death in the presence of the King, on the North Inch in Perth.

It was a bloody struggle and at its conclusion the last remaining Cameron leapt into the Tay and escaped. The 11 Clan Chattan survivors were presented – battered, bloody, but triumphant – to King Robert, who judged them the winners. The battle quietened the feud for many decades.

This battle also provides the time and place for two new strands to Clan Chattan. The clan was led, at the North Inch, by Shaw, the son of the Mackintosh chief. As a reward for victory, his father gave him the lands of Rothiemurchus, where he and his descendants became known as Clan Shaw.

Just prior to the battle at the North Inch, it was discovered that Clan Chattan was, for whatever reason, one man short. A local Perth armourer smith called Gow (Smith in Gaelic is *Gobha*) volunteered and fought very fiercely with Clan Chattan. He was thereafter adopted into the clan, and the names of Smith and Gow appear from that time forward.

In 1409, the tenth Mackintosh chief came to power. His name was Malcolm, and Clan Chattan grew in numbers and territory under his leadership. He married Mora MacDonald of Clanranald and, as was the custom, she brought with her many kinsmen from Moidart. This is why we see Clan Chattan henceforth including MacAndrew, Gillanders and Macqueen. In fact it would be one of these Macqueens who reputedly killed the last wolf in Scotland, just east of Moy, centuries later in 1743.

In 1424, the feud with the Comyns reignited. Alexander Comyn took, and hanged, a number of Mackintosh men. In retaliation Malcolm slew some of Comyn's landed followers in the Castle of

Nairn. The Comyns then raised a considerable force and invaded the Mackintosh clanlands. It is said the Mackintoshes took refuge on the island in Loch Moy, upon which there was a village and chiefly residence at the time. The Comyns dammed the loch outflow to flood the Mackintosh island.

There was one clansman who was a particularly strong swimmer, so he swam, in dark of night, to the dam. There, with aid of rope and axe, he demolished the structure, washing away the army of Comyns camped beneath on the riverbank. He was tragically drowned along with his enemies.

The Comyns pretended reconciliation while plotting revenge. They invited the Mackintoshes to a feast at Rait Castle but planned to kill their guests on the signal of a bull's head being carried in. Comyn's daughter was in love with a Mackintosh lad and, although sworn to secrecy, told the details to *only* the stone at the lovers' meeting place near the castle – the boulder is still called 'The Stone of the Maiden' to this day. Thus she was not breaking her oath, even if her sweetheart, who she knew would be behind the rock, happened to overhear the plan.

Immediately the bull's head appeared, therefore, each Mackintosh fell upon a Comyn. The chief of the Comyns survived long enough to run to his daughter's bedchamber, suspecting her of the betrayal. When she saw his fury, she attempted escape through her window. As she hung there, he, enraged, cut off both her hands with one sweep of his broadsword.

Having finally broken the Comyns' grip on their lands, Malcolm, Captain of Clan Chattan, obtained a charter for both Rait and Meikle Geddes that year, 1442. However, local tradition relates that from the night on which the massacre and tragedy was enacted, the bloodstained walls of Rait have been tenantless and the apparition of a girl with no hands is sometimes seen in the vicinity.

A branch of the MacLeans, from Lochbuie on Mull, had come

north around 1400 as Constables of Urquhart Castle. They became known as the MacLeans of Dochgarroch and were assimilated into Clan Chattan on their chief's marriage to Malcolm's daughter, Margaret. At about this same time, the Clarks sought recognition by the confederation. Before the close of the fifteenth century, they were joined by two other septs, as new members. The MacThomases, who descended from the Mackintosh seventh chief, and the Badenoch MacIntyres, who were the family of a MacIntyre bard who sought the protection of Clan Chattan in 1496.

Clan Chattan fell foul of James V in 1528, when the young King assumed the reins of power for the first time. When Lachlan, 14th chief of Mackintosh, was murdered at the Findhorn in 1526, his infant son was taken charge of by the boy's uncle, the Earl of Moray. Clan Chattan took offence and, led by another uncle, Hector Mackintosh, temporary captain of Clan Chattan, they attacked the Earl of Moray, burned the town of Dyke and laid waste the Earl's lands in Moray.

In response, the King's decree was 'to pass upon the Clan Chattan and invade them to their utter destruction by slaughtering, burning, drowning and other ways, and leave no creature living of that clan except priests, women and bairns'.

Thankfully for all concerned, the Earl of Moray decided, at the last minute, to take some responsibility for having begun the unrest. He suspended the order and things eventually quietened down.

It is said that the confederation's first bond of mutual support was created in 1397, after the Battle of the North Inch. That document became lost and so, early in the seventeenth century, it was decided to renew it with a new document, 'The Bond of Union'.

Thus, on the chilly morning of 4 April 1609, chiefs from the various Clan Chattan septs met at a house called Termit, on Petty Ridge. Termit was probably chosen as it had the largest walled garden at Petty. The affair was solemn and well attended, and the paperwork still exists to this day, bearing all of the names of the signatories and also of the Inverness provost, the burgh clerk and the Petty minister, who were all called upon as witnesses.

Termit was to disappear some 200 years later, swept away by the agricultural reorganisation that broke up cottages and gardens and incorporated them into large new fields. The location of the signing of this bond became, thereafter, part of Morayston Farm.

The renewal of the bond of mutual support was also a direct response to both regional and national political manoeuvrings. Regionally, Mackintosh had lost two chiefs to violence in the previous century, leading to troublesome minorities. This was compounded by the recent rise in power of George, 6th Earl of Huntly. George's politicking bore fruit in 1591 when he obtained a Bond of Friendship with Andrew MacPherson of Cluny and encouraged him to make a play for leadership of Clan Chattan. It was to help heal this breach, therefore, that the clan was renewing their bonds of loyalty.

Nationally, James VI, just six years earlier, had become James I of England too, moving his court to London. James had never been a particular admirer of Highland culture and the farther he distanced himself from it, the more he seemed to view it as barbarous and unacceptable.

It was not long before fears about King James's plans seemed justified. Just four months later, in August 1609, James's commissioner, the Bishop of the Isles, drew up a list of statutes for many of the west coast chiefs to sign.

There were nine statutes in total, which included prohibitions on the bearing of arms, a ban on receiving Bards and on any buying or selling of any wine or whisky, conformation to the discipline of the reformed Kirk and the necessity for all folk of substance to send their eldest sons and daughters south to be educated in English. These were known as the Statutes of Iona and can easily be seen as the precursor to all of the various acts of Parliament which would be enacted upon the Highlanders throughout the years of the eighteenth century.

Meanwhile, there were still a number of significant armed conflicts awaiting the clan later in the seventeenth century (including fighting with Montrose's forces in support of Charles I). The Bond of Union was renewed in 1664 and extended to include the Farquharsons for the first time. They were a related family who descended from the Shaws of Rothiemurchus (who, as has been said, descend in turn from the Mackintosh that commanded at the Battle of the North Inch). The Farquharsons were the last major addition to the Clan of the Cat and brought to full strength the confederation which would go on to fiercely defend the rights of the Stuart dynasty in the next century.

In 1665, the Mackintoshes, under Lachlan, their 19th chief, met with the Camerons, led by Ewen, their 17th chief. There were over a thousand men on each side and a stand-off ensued near Achnacarry. But at the last minute, bloodshed was averted. Even more miraculously, handshakes were given and promises made. Weapons were even exchanged as a sign of good faith, and there ended what was often called the longest and bloodiest feud in Highland history. It had been running for 360 years!

Lachlan's troubles, thereafter, were mainly with MacDonell of Keppoch, and the last ever clan battle in the Highlands took place between their forces at Mulroy in 1688. In the national struggle for the throne, in 1688 and 1689, Lachlan Mackintosh, although sympathetic to James VII and II, would not rise. This was due to Viscount Dundee's dealings with Keppoch.

As the seventeenth century passed quietly into the eighteenth, Lachlan, finding Dalcross Castle inconvenient for some reason, chose to build a new home. He decided to site it back on the fourteenth-century ancestral lands at Moy. He built Moy Hall at the north end of Loch Moy and, by 1702 an elderly man, made over his estates to his son. He died in 1704 and his body lay in state for a month. When he was finally buried, at Petty, 2,000 armed men attended the funeral. Due to the turnout of all of the neighbouring chiefs and their followers, it is said that the funeral procession extended for four miles.

| Old Clan Chattan | Mackintosh and related | For Mutual Support | Now Extinct |
|---|---|---|---|
| MacPherson | Mackintosh | MacGillivray | Tarrill |
| Davidson | Shaw | MacBean | Clan Dhu |
| MacPhail | MacLean | Gow | Sliochd MacAonas |
| | MacAndrew | Clark | Gorries |
| | Macqueen | MacIntyre | |
| | MacThomas | | |
| | Farquharson | | |

*Summary of the principal branches of the Clan Chattan*

## Upland Worship

The church of Barevan is found nestling high in the hills east of Cantraydoune. The earliest feues relating to this church of St Evan (or Ewen) date from 1239 and the building itself probably the fourteenth century. Thus it is the oldest pre-Reformation chapel in the area. Looking westwards from the churchyard, you can see a low hill rise just one field away. It forms a level green prominence called Drumournie, which means 'the Hill of Prayer'. Could this have been the site of St Ewen's early sermons?

Many of the Thanes of Cawdor are interred in Barevan churchyard. It is a peaceful setting but, although there was a village (or clachan) nearby when the church was in use, there is no house in sight. The building has unique Norman-arched windows, an unusual double-basined piscina (just where the altar stood) and a couple of arched doors (one with an old draw-bar socket).

This cemetery was not just a place for burials; it was also the place for penance and punishment. Even today the open stone coffin can be seen, near the church wall, under the trees. Imagine the terror, in those superstitious times, of being forced to stay in the darkened churchyard all night. There, the mischief-maker would lie, imprisoned by a heavy lid of stone slab, covering feet to chin and held down on the coffin by the large stone ball, still there, and alleged to weigh 18 stone (252 lbs).

Worship underwent a radical change at Barevan due to the Reformation, which had its origins as early as 1520, with Lutheran leaflets entering Scotland through east coast ports such as Inverness. The change culminated in 1560, when a Scottish Parliament abolished Roman Catholicism.

It was unfortunate that the religious change sweeping Europe coincided with a time of political instability in Scotland. James V had died young, leaving his newborn daughter, Mary, Queen of Scots as heir to the throne. The religious reformers rose in arms, demanding that Mary be betrothed to Henry VIII of England's son and heir. Mary's mother, the Regent, was French and Catholic and favoured a betrothal to the Dauphin of France. Thus religious and political factors polarised with the Protestant pro-English faction set against the Catholic pro-French faction of the Queen Mother. This was the beginning of the troubles which would, in the fullness of time, see Mary, and later her great-grandson, James VII and II, lose the throne. The wars involving Charles I, and a century later Bonnie Prince Charlie, centred more on the contention between Episcopacy and Presbyterianism. All this was yet to come.

Meanwhile, Barevan was, until the seventeenth century, the centre of a parish which included the village of Cawdor. Barevan church was adopted and used by the Protestant faith until 1619. When the Thane of Cawdor at that time, John Roy Campbell, nearly drowned in a great storm off the island of Islay, he prayed for deliverance. Saved, he decided to give thanks by building a new church in Cawdor. That church's doors opened in 1619. Andrew Balfour, the last minister who preached at Barevan, closed his upland chapel for a final time, moving the ministering business downhill. The parish was then renamed Cawdor.

Barevan slumbers peacefully for the most part now. Visiting this secluded haven, it can be hard to bring to mind those troubled times during the seventeenth and eighteenth centuries. This place is a sanctuary, a place of rest, and others obviously think so too. Walking to the north wall, at the back of the churchyard, it is possible to view the new area enclosed by the current family at Cawdor. The most recent Thane to pass away is buried here. His memorial names him: Hugh Campbell, the 6th Earl and the 24th Thane. A striking new monument echoes the stone ball in the churchyard and carved upon it is a plea for all those who lie within Barevan's walls: 'Lord Jesus Christ and son of God, have mercy upon me and all who rest here.'

## That Man, Callum Beg

The lands of Cawdor, just eight miles from Culloden, were, in the mid-seventeenth century, also held by a Sir Hugh Campbell of Cawdor. These lands occupied a large swathe of Nairnshire, including much of the valleys of the Rivers Nairn and Findhorn.

It is said that a certain tenant of Sir Hugh's was a notorious cattle reiver. This rogue was called Callum Beg – although it isn't known whether he was the inspiration for Sir Walter Scott's character by the same name in his novel, *Waverley*.

He lived in the upland reaches of the Findhorn Valley, in an area called the Streens. His cottage was on the north bank, just upstream from Banchor, on a particularly wild stretch of the river. From this mountain fastness, he would make his raids on the lower lands nearer the sea, making off with the very best of the cattle.

His close neighbours always referred to him as 'that honest man, Callum Beg!' There are at least two possible reasons for this. It may have been due to the fact that he had a reputation for generosity: it was said that 'Callum never killed a beast but he shared it with his friends'. Then again, there was his stature. The name 'Callum Beg' means 'wee Callum', which was nothing but a wry joke. Stories describe this freebooter as huge: 'a giant in strength, [he] could carry a weight of booty slung over his shoulders which would crush any ordinary man'.

This cattle reiver must have been personable, however, as well as lawless and bold, as he was apparently well thought of and a great favourite with his landlord, Hugh of Cawdor. In fact he was often asked to accompany the laird, as gillie and companion, on hunting and fishing trips in the hills, and sometimes Sir Hugh would make a holiday of it and stay with Callum for some days. This is a practice which has been formalised by later generations of the family in the building of a hunting lodge at Drynachan, just along the valley.

One particular year, Sir Hugh arrived, unusually in the grumpiest of moods, for his week-long stay at the Streens. He had been put completely out of sorts by the theft of the best bullock in his herd at Cawdor Castle just the night before. There was no trail to follow and there were no likely suspects.

Every morning, he bemoaned to Callum the loss of so fine an animal, and every day, as they sat down to lunch, more complaints would be forthcoming. The usually carefree expeditions on the hills and moors were morose affairs, until Callum, unable to stand Sir Hugh's dejection a minute longer, found the truth bursting from him: 'Laird, laird, ye need na mak' sae much din about it, for ye have had your ain share of the beast!' Callum had been feeding Sir Hugh with his own stolen bullock on a daily basis since he got there!

Streens is a fair stretch from Cawdor Castle. It is about a dozen miles, over some fairly high country, and on foot would ordinarily be a journey of some hours. This was why, on one unusually stormy night, when Callum had arrived at the castle in order to pay his rent, he was invited to stay overnight. He was told that he would share the bed with the farm manager.

Callum ensured that a drink or two before bed had his companion sleeping soundly. Then, during the night, he got up, chose a nice fat animal from the castle herds, drove it across the hills to his cottage on the Findhorn and managed to get back, long before his bedmate stirred.

Next day, the castle was in uproar about the missing beast. But the one thing that the farm manager would not hear of was that Callum Beg might have had anything to do with it. 'Oh, no!' he said, 'that honest man, Callum Beg, was sleeping soundly at my side throughout the night.'

The towns from Inverness to Elgin were known, in times past, for their cattle markets and were among Callum's regular hunting grounds. There was more than one suspicious glance cast whenever he went to market.

One day, while visiting the Forres market, he spotted a likely beast – very tempting, if not for one distinguishing feature. It had no tail. He found this more than a little off-putting, as he generally found that stealing cattle went better when not taking animals that were readily identifiable. This would be harder than usual . . .

Next morning saw him driving a cow from Forres to Nairn, and being stopped and accused by the enraged owner of the lost cow.

'Had your beast a tail like that?' asked Callum.

'No,' came the baffled reply, 'my beast had no tail at all.'

'Well, then,' said a delighted Callum, 'that's an end to it.' Then off he went, westwards, no doubt blessing his sewing skills under his breath and wondering when it might be noticed that someone had stolen the tail from another cow in the market during the night!

A life of freebooting had its hazards, and its narrow escapes.

On one occasion, Callum was actually caught red-handed with a stolen sheep. He was brought before Sir Hugh, who was placed in a situation of needing to be seen to dispense judgement but wishing to protect his favoured tenant.

After some thought, he ordered Callum and the sheep to be put in the dungeon, and the complainers to be fed and given ale. While they ate, the laird slipped a message to the dungeon. He hoped that Callum had a good knife and promised customers for the sheep. Not slow at catching on, Callum killed and butchered the sheep, throwing the portions out of the dungeon via the air ducts. The pack of hounds, waiting eagerly outside, made short work of the remains.

Finally, the laird took to the judgement chair, calling for the thief, the stolen property and witnesses to be presented. The witnesses filed in and Callum was fetched from the dungeon, but there was no sign, of course, of the sheep, of which not one chop could be found. There was a certain inevitability about the ruling – the witnesses were charged with conspiring against 'that honest man, Callum Beg' and, accordingly, the prisoner was set free.

There were few estates on Nairnside and Strathnairn that did not suffer at the hands of this cattle thief at some point. Sir Hugh's neighbour, the laird of Kilravock Castle (pronounced 'Kilrock'), lived about five miles east of Culloden. He found these raids to be very infuriating, so was more than pleased when Callum Beg was finally delivered into his hands and imprisoned by him.

Sir Hugh, hearing of Callum's predicament, racked his brains for a solution and remembered an age-old tradition. He made haste to Kilravock Castle on New Year's Day and waited at the doors. He was, of course, invited in but replied that he had a New Year's boon to ask and unless it were granted he would not enter the house or partake of his neighbour's hospitality.

'I shall grant you every favour in my power,' replied Kilravock, 'but the life of Callum Beg.'

Sir Hugh, looking into that resolute face, saw no chance of his changing his mind and so, regretfully, he departed, leaving Callum to his ultimate fate. Kilravock wasted little time in sentencing Callum and ensuring that he paid for his crimes at the end of a rope.

In the nineteenth century, a skeleton of appropriate size was dug up nearby, with a noose around its neck. The local folk identified this as the body of 'that cattle reiver, Callum Beg!'

## Croy – A Highland Parish

Drummossie Moor sits just on the western edge of the Parish of Croy. There are two ancient estates within the parish: Kilravock, as we have heard, the seat of the chiefs of Clan Rose, and Holme Rose, one of their smaller holdings upstream.

Rose of Kilravock also kept a town house in the nearby Royal Burgh of Nairn. Their close links with the town were clearly shown by the fact that 46 out of the 47 provosts of Nairn, between 1450 and 1777, were Roses. The one that wasn't was Major James Clephane . . . and he was a brother-in-law substitute, after whom the Kilravock estate village of Clephanton is named.

The parish is an old one, and to the west of the church is a large, grey stone called Clach na Seanaish, or listening stone, at which, in earlier centuries, secret meetings took place about the movements and designs of hostile clans. The parish was joined with Dalcross in the fifteenth century. Croy village sits in a lovely spot and has been a good place for generations of folk to live. The Statistical Accounts of 1820, however, hint that, for a short while, it was a different tale:

> From 1640 . . . the parish records were kept with singular care . . . This parish was certainly then ranked with every species of abomination. In the black catalogue, besides the sin of uncleanness, may be mentioned – drying and grinding corn and killing salmon on the Sabbath; brawling, drunkenness and fighting in church; defamation of character; fighting at lykwakes [watching

over a dead body]; casting the sieve and the sheers
[superstitious method to catch a thief]; and not a few
for endeavouring to compass their neighbour's death by
charms, spells, and many kindred follies. The cutty-stool
got little rest.

Time, and the removal of their bigamous minister in 1700, seemed
to quieten Croy down again – until national affairs intruded almost
another half-century later.

## A Time of Omens, a Gift of Sight

Precognition, or second sight, has always been an accepted part of
Highland culture. The ability to 'see', in the sense of foretelling the
future, or to 'see' an occurrence which is happening miles away is
a talent said to run in Highland families. Those who have these
visions have, in the past, been called 'seers' – and while some of
them considered this ability as a talent or gift, others saw it as a
curse.

Reverend John Morrison was the most famous seer to live near
Drummossie. He was the minister in the Parish of Petty from 1759
until 1774, and due to his visionary predictions he became known
as the Petty Seer.

He foretold the Petty clearances by saying, 'Large as the ridge
of Petty is, and thickly as it is now populated, the day will come,
and is not far off, when there will only be three smokes in it,
and the crow of the cock at each cannot be heard, owing to the
distance, at either of the others.' This occurred through the loss
of smallholdings as they were combined to create large farms like
Morayston.

The Reverend also thundered during a sermon: 'Ye sinful and
stiff-necked people, God will, unless ye turn from your evil ways,
sweep you ere long into the place of torment; and as a sign of what
I say, *Clach Dubh an Abain,* large though it be, will be carried soon

without human agency a considerable distance seawards.'

This happened a mere 26 years later, in February 1799. This stone, located on the south side of the bay of Petty and weighing over eight tons, moved overnight, about 260 yards down into the sea. One explanation was that the ice around the boulder (18 in. thick) had been lifted, together with the stone, by the tide during the hurricane that had hit on the night in question. Today, the stone can be seen at low tide from Old Petty Church.

The Petty Seer lived in the latter half of the eighteenth century, many years after the Jacobite rising. The greatest and best known of all the Highland seers, the Brahan Seer, lived at least 100 years earlier, probably in the latter half of the seventeenth century. There is, however, a contrary argument that he lived in the sixteenth century and some documentation has come to light which may support that fact. Either way there is a whole body of predictive statements attributed to him and these are often grouped in three types: those prophecies which have come to pass; those prophecies which are partially fulfilled; and, most intriguing of all, those prophecies which have yet to be fulfilled. So who was this man?

Some accounts have him originally being a native of the island of Lewis, although whether from Ness or the Parish of Uig is unproven. Others suggest Easter Ross. Wherever he was from, the tales generally agree that he took work as a field labourer on the Brahan Estate.

His name was Kenneth Mackenzie, but Gaelic tradition records him as Coinneach Odhar, which translates as Dun or Brown Kenneth, probably a reference to hair colour. The title Brahan Seer was not used until coined by Alexander Mackenzie as a book title in 1877.

He made at least three predictions about Culloden which have been documented. The first prophecy was about a shadow covering Culloden. The second was a more specific offering, in which he said: 'the day will come when the wheel at Millburn will be turned for three successive days with water red with human blood; for on the lade's bank a fierce battle shall be fought in which much blood will be spilt'.

A seer without parallel in the Highlands, his talent was strong, and his predictions were bold. His prophecies were also often recorded in writing, generations before their fulfilment. The Brahan Seer is still known today and his predictions remain cause for heated discussion.

Not everyone believes in second sight, however. Some people think that it represents intelligent guesswork and anticipation by clever people using deductive reasoning, and then pretending that they have a psychic talent.

The Brahan Seer, for example, predicted that 'the time will come, and it is not far off, when full-rigged ships will be seen sailing eastward and westward by the back of Tomnahurich, near Inverness'. This was a full century and a half before the Caledonian Canal was constructed, passing the foot of Tomnahurich Hill. A case *could* be made that knowledge of geography, and of economics, might allow such a conclusion to be reached independent of supernatural means. Then again, there are a whole range of predictions that defy rational or everyday explanation.

His third prophecy concerning Culloden is a perfect example of this. He was travelling on some business in the area and while passing across Drummossie ridge, on the moor road, was taken poorly, calling, 'Oh! Drummossie, thy bleak moor shall, ere many generations have passed away, be stained with the best blood of the Highlands. Glad I am that I will not see that day, for it will be a fearful period; heads will be lopped off by the score, and no mercy will be shown or quarter given on either side.'

This shadow on the moor, foreseen by the Brahan Seer, was to fall, deep and black, in the next century. It was chilling just how accurately this prediction would be fulfilled.

# PART TWO

# TALES FROM THE BATTLE

**When the King Enjoys His Own Again**

Let rogues and cheats prognosticate
Concerning king's or kingdom's fate
I think myself to be as wise
As he that gazeth on the skies
My sight goes beyond
The depth of a pond
Or rivers in the greatest rain
Whereby I can tell
That all will be well
When the King enjoys his own again

*Yes, this I can tell*
*That all will be well*
*When the King enjoys his own again*

– Anonymous

# Register of Tales

# The Road to Drummossie Moor

And so it begins – an inexorable slide towards the mayhem and carnage that has already been foretold by the Brahan Seer. Politics, culture, religion and the blind fates themselves weave a complex dance that brings us ever closer to the events that burn the name Culloden forever into the psyche of three continents.

The House of Stewart had been the ruling dynasty in Scotland since 1371 and many of these monarchs had mixed feelings about the clan culture in the Highlands. It was just too different for Lowland Scotland to accept. While most of Britain had adopted the laws, customs and practices of the feudal Norman south, the Highlands had retained the systems of the ancient Celtic realm. The Highlanders were, as a consequence, a deeply honour-bound society, and this was one source of the ambivalence in their relationship with the King of Scots through the centuries. He was *their* King, and their loyalty was both fierce and extravagant.

The monarch, however, lived mainly in the Norman society, which couldn't understand or accept the Highland way of life and saw the clans as a dark threat, lying just beyond the civilised bounds – the 'wild men' in the north.

By the time Mary, Queen of Scots ascended the throne in 1542, the Stewarts had ruled for nearly two centuries. (She had lived in France for 13 years and, since there was no letter 'W' in the French language at that time, is the monarch sometimes credited with changing the spelling to 'Stuart' for easier usage in her adoptive home.) Her son was crowned James VI of Scotland in 1567, at the age of one.

On the night of 24 March 1603, a messenger, having ridden from London in three days, brought James news that Elizabeth I of England was dead. Two days later, word reached him that the Privy Council had declared him her successor. The Stuart dynasty continued to rule thereafter, as monarchs under the united crowns of Scotland and England.

James VII and II came to the throne in 1685. James had been raised in the Protestant faith, like his father and grandfather before him. This is why Mary and Anne, the daughters from his first marriage, were also Protestant. James converted to Catholicism just before the death of his first wife, Anne Hyde, and then married Mary of Modena. Eleven pregnancies later, in June 1688, she was delivered of a healthy son: a Catholic heir to the throne.

This was one step too far for some of the already troubled Protestant nobility. Seven of them wrote to William of Orange in Holland (William was James's nephew, as well as the husband of James's daughter, Mary). They offered an invitation for him to invade, which he accepted, and William landed on the south coast of England with an army in November 1688.

James VII and II fled to France in fear for his life, and the Jacobite era can be said to have begun then (the term Jacobite merely means a follower of James, or Jacobus, as it is in Latin).

William and Mary ruled jointly, and William later came to an accommodation with Parliament to prevent his brother-in-law, James, from ascending the throne after his death. This accommodation, called the Act of Settlement, precluded any Catholic from taking the throne. Mary's sister therefore became the next monarch in line and was crowned Queen Anne in 1702. Indeed it was she who was responsible for nicknaming James 'The Pretender'.

Anne died in 1714, and the Act of Settlement ensured that her successor was George, the Elector of Hanover (another great-grandson of James VI and I).

The decades between 1688 and 1719 saw four major attempts to restore first James VII and II, then later his son, to the throne. These risings were influenced by broader European politics and at different times received French and/or Spanish help.

Then in 1745, James VII and II's grandson, Charles Edward Stuart, landed in the Highlands and raised his standard at Glenfinnan, 15 miles west of Fort William. His intention was to win back the throne for his father, who, although in exile in Paris, had already been recognised by Stuart adherents, in 1701, as King James VIII and III of Great Britain.

Moving fast and decisively, the Jacobites smashed government forces at Prestonpans and then advanced deep into England, reaching Derby, just a couple of days' march from London. There, due to dissension in the Jacobite command structure and government misinformation, the decision was taken to return to Scotland.

Four months later, Bonnie Prince Charlie and his forces were in Inverness, while the government forces had over-wintered at Aberdeen. The government forces were led by William Augustus, Duke of Cumberland, who was the favoured son of King George II. King George had been crowned King of Great Britain in London in 1727.

On 15 April, these two armies began closing, commanded by two cousins, each representing their respective fathers' claims to the British throne. Obviously aware of the shortcomings of Drummossie Moor as a battle site, the Jacobites chose to attempt a night march to Nairn and a surprise attack on the government camp. However, the night of the 15th was moonless and, defeated by darkness and distance, the Jacobites failed to reach their objective and had to struggle back to Drummossie.

When the Jacobite army did finally face Cumberland across 500 yards of moorland at 11 a.m. on Wednesday, 16 April 1746, most had not eaten for more than two days and were exhausted. They were on ground ideally suited to the government forces' artillery and which was totally unsuited to the Highland charge. The Jacobites on the field numbered at most 5,000 men, while the government army facing them was perhaps 9,000 strong.

# MacDonald of Clanranald

Nine months before Culloden, Prince Charles's first footfall on Scottish soil was on the Clanranald island of Eriskay. There, MacDonald of Boisdale advised him to return home, and he uttered the now famous phrase, 'I am come home.'

In 1745, Clanranald still had large territories on the western coast and the Prince landed next on another of their holdings, on the mainland. The chief took no active part in the rising, but his son Ranald MacDonald, 'Young Clanranald', was a firm supporter from the start. Clanranalds comprised the Prince's initial bodyguard of fifty men and later provided three companies at the raising of the standard at Glenfinnan on 19 August.

Commanded by Young Clanranald, the regiment began by taking Dundee and its shipping. They were in the thick of the action at Prestonpans and later accompanied the Prince to Derby. They were at their best strength, about 350 men, at the Battle of Falkirk on 17 January 1746.

Unfortunately, just three days after this battle, one of Clanranald's men was cleaning his gun when it accidentally went off. The ball passed through the window and, by the worst of chances, killed Colonel Angus MacDonell on the street outside. He was the well-liked and admired leader of MacDonell of Glengarry's Regiment, as well as being the chief's son. The Glengarrys required the life of the luckless Clanranald, so dragged him to a wall where his own father delivered the killing shot to give him a quick passing. As a result of these events, both regiments became unsettled, leading to desertions. They may also partially explain why the Clanranald Regiment fielded only about 200 men at Culloden, on the left of the line, with the other MacDonalds.

Their casualties were very high: Young Clanranald was badly wounded and many others were taken prisoner. Like the Prince himself, the clansmen who survived the battle struggled westwards to begin fugitive lives in the heather. When the Prince left five months later, his departure – like his arrival – was from Clanranald lands.

# MacDonell of Keppoch

As I stand here, on this open ground, looking east, the wind is bitter and I can feel the touch of ice along the edges of my bones. This ground is not good for our charge. But I will do what I can, for the Prince, and for my Chief.

Our traditional place of honour on the right, given to us by Robert the Bruce, after Bannockburn, has been taken by the Athollmen. For our Prince, we have agreed to this place on the left. The line here is not straight, though, so we shall have far further to run than the other regiments, and much of the field in front of us is low, flat and covered with water to the depth of our knees, so I cannot see how that shall be. But we will strive to our utmost.

I am a captain in my father's regiment, and am called Angus Ban of Inch. Though Keppoch is my father, hopefully I will never have to lead the clan, being only a natural son. I am, however, determined to make him proud today.

Alexander MacDonell, my father, is the 17th Chief of the MacDonalds of Keppoch. He matriculated at the University of Glasgow in 1713, where he studied until leaving to join his own father, and the Jacobite forces, in the 1715 rising. Exiled to the Continent, he then served as an officer in the French Army. He was allowed to return to Scotland in 1719, and settled, for a time, at Waternish in Skye. It was there that he had a union with my mother. She was a weaver, but I was never to know her, as she died during my infancy.

My father returned to Keppoch about 1729, where he managed to live quietly until now. Last year he raised his men to join the Prince at Glenfinnan, in August.

Since then we have been almost the length of this island Kingdom. Most recently, the Prince sent us to besiege Fort William, and we only returned to his side, here at Culloden, last night. And now, here we stand, 200 strong, awaiting the call to action.

The ice on my bones turned to stone in my belly. We were defeated. We made a brave attempt, all of the MacDonald Regiments. So much went wrong. The order to charge came too late, and the ground stopped us building the power needed to smash the redcoat ranks. All we could do was come close, and try to tempt them to action. We tried this tactic three times, coming to under a hundred yards of them, but all to no avail. And then the right and centre retired in full flight, and all we could do was follow them, because our right flank was then open to raking fire.

Donald Roy MacDonald saw my father caught in the deadly grapeshot and falling. He found the strength to shout to Donald, 'O God, have mercy upon me! Donald, do the best for yourself, for I am gone.' So commanded, Donald Roy ran on.

James MacDonell, a captain like me, came upon my father, and seeing that it was only his arm that was shattered, he helped him up, but as they struggled back, a second shot hit Keppoch in the back, and he fell again. James checked for signs of life. Seeing none, he left him.

By this time we were all in full flight, and the next two men to recognise their chief, where he lay, were Angus Ferguson and John MacInnes. Their stories were so similar there is no reason to doubt either. Both thought Keppoch to be dead, and bore witness to his shattered right arm and fatal chest wound – from back through to front.

I was next to pass, and felt my heart like to break when I saw him. But he wasn't gone. He rallied a little, and my companions and I lifted him and got him clear of the field. 'We will dress his wounds, and then try to get him home,' I said. We took him to a nearby hut, filled with many of the wounded from the field, but by the time we laid him down, he was dead.

Unlooked for, I was now Tutor of Keppoch, required to lead the clan during my half-brother's minority. I acted as my father would have wished, saving such of our people as I could, from that field of death. I took his sword and dirk home, and hid them near to Keppoch House.

I went to the meeting of the chiefs at Achnacarry on the 8th of May, where we entered into a bond of mutual defence in our now perilous situation. We were the last of the clans to lay down arms. Capitulation became inevitable when the enemy invaded our glens. Keppoch House was burned on the 3rd of June, and I took my father's family into hiding. His colours were burned at Glasgow Mercat Cross on the 25th of June and, in many ways, that was the true end of the rising for us.

Sometimes, in my mind, I see the boulder, marking the place of my father's fall, and I think 'Take this burden back! I only want he who has gone to be restored to us.'

Based on the accounts of Angus Ban and other members of the Keppoch Regiment.

*The Keppoch Stone*

# MacDonell of Glengarry

This was one of the largest regiments in the Prince's army. It included the Grants and Mackenzies of Glenmoriston and Glenurquhart, as well as MacLeod of Raasay and MacDonell of Barrisdale.

The chief, John MacDonell of Glengarry, did not accompany them. He was quite infirm and was said to have an alcohol problem. His eldest son, Alasdair Ruadh MacDonell, was in France, and so it was the chief's cousin, Donald of Lochgarry, who raised the regiment. The commander was Glengarry's second son, Angus. Another cousin to the chief, MacDonell of Scotus, brought 50 men to the regiment.

Alasdair Ruadh did attempt to return from France to join the Prince, but his ship, together with the troops that were with him, were all captured in early November and Alasdair was imprisoned in the Tower of London until July 1747.

Glengarry's Regiment took part in the march to Derby and was in the hottest of the action at the Battle of Clifton during the retreat north. The regiment was reinforced on its return to Scotland and fielded around a thousand men at Falkirk. Then, as has been related, they lost their well-liked colonel through mischance and Glengarry's third son, James, took over, although in name only: command remained with Lochgarry.

By late February, the Jacobites were back in the Inverness area. MacDonell of Scotus had, during the campaign, become firm friends with James Johnstone, the Chevalier de Johnstone, who later wrote full memoirs.

On 19 March, it was decided to gather a flotilla of small boats at Findhorn to carry more than a thousand men to Sutherland to engage Lord Loudon's government forces at their headquarters in Dornoch. Scotus and his men had been chosen to take part in this raid, but the news brought him only grief. Johnstone's memoirs make clear that when he asked his friend what was wrong,

Scotus answered that his son, Ranald, was an officer in Loudon's Regiment:

> Perhaps, tomorrow, I may be so unfortunate as to kill my son with my own hand; and thus the same ball which I fire in my defence may give to myself the most cruel death! However, in going with the detachment, I may be able to save him, and if I do not go, he may fall to the hands of another.

This mission, at least, had a happy outcome. When Scotus and Johnstone met on the raiding party's return, Scotus was overjoyed to introduce Ranald, who, against the odds, he had indeed managed to capture without mishap. The three of them spent a pleasant and convivial evening, dining at the Chevalier's apartment.

About a hundred of Loudon's men were taken prisoner during this raid, and perhaps the most well known was the chief of Clan Mackintosh, Aeneas, who, as will soon be told, was given into his wife's custody at Moy.

Around three weeks later, the entire Jacobite army was drawn up on Drummossie Moor. Glengarry's Regiment was about 500 strong. Scotus was there, and Johnstone said that when the order came to advance, they all got to within 20 paces of the enemy. But it was slow going, with water halfway up their legs, and so, lacking both running momentum and that thunderous impact, there was no hope of success. Many fell, including Scotus and 22 of his band. He was being carried off the field by a couple of his men when he saw some dragoons closing in on them. He knew his wound was mortal, so told them to leave him and save themselves. He asked only to be left facing the enemy, so they wouldn't think he was running away.

Lochgarry got clear of the field, later escaping to France with the Prince, but old Glengarry was imprisoned and his castle burnt.

About a year later, Alasdair Ruadh was released from the Tower and eventually became the next Glengarry in 1754.

## The Clan Donald Stone

As outlined in the MacDonell of Keppoch piece, all the MacDonald Regiments ran into heavy fire, and losses, out on the left of the line. Those who fell were buried where they lay. This was because the main grave pits were thought to be too far away for the young country folk on the burial parties to carry the bodies. The Clan Donald Society erected their memorial stone in the general vicinity of the fallen to honour Clanranald, Glengarry, Keppoch, Glencoe and all the other cadet branches of the MacDonalds who had members in the battle.

*The Clan Donald Stone*

## Clan Cameron

Clan Cameron's homeland is Lochaber, and they were ever loyal to the House of Stewart. The 18th chief, John Cameron, fought in both the 1715 and the 1719 risings, and lived in exile thereafter. His son, Donald Cameron of Lochiel (known as 'the Gentle Lochiel'), then led the clan as the 19th chief, though his father was still alive.

Lochiel was a civilised and cultured individual and probably one of the most highly respected chiefs in the Highlands. Where the chief of the Camerons led, other clans often followed. This was why many other chiefs agreed with Lochiel when he took the view that there would need to be substantial French backing, arms, supplies and several thousand soldiers before the clans would consider rising. Armed conflict seemed unlikely, therefore, and the Highlands would have remained quiet but for two factors. First, the government foolishly backed Lochiel into a corner, in June, by issuing a warrant for his arrest (on the basis of incriminating papers that had come into their hands) and, secondly, Bonnie Prince Charlie decided to come 'ower the water' in person and throw himself on the chivalry and loyalty of the chiefs.

Lochiel first met Prince Charles in Moidart on 30 July, though the content of their discussion will forever be a mystery. Not even Charles was sure whether he had won Lochiel's support. Three weeks later the Prince waited anxiously at Glenfinnan, with his small force of MacDonalds. The hours slid slowly by, then, with true Highland drama and a sense of timing, the strains of the pipes were heard and the 800 Camerons came marching over the braes. The 1745 rising had begun.

One of Lochiel's younger brothers was Doctor Archibald Cameron. Prior to the rising, he had studied in Glasgow, Edinburgh and Paris, and had returned to the Highlands well qualified to improve the health of the people. Although not a man of warlike nature, he was nevertheless willing to do what he saw as his duty when the Prince landed. He became a lieutenant colonel, physician and aide-de-camp in the Jacobite army. He was at both Prestonpans and Falkirk (being wounded in the latter engagement). Throughout the campaign he tended both Jacobite and captured Hanoverian wounded with equal care, and became loved and respected throughout the Jacobite army.

Doctor Archie was also present at the Battle of Culloden. He would have seen the loss of many clansmen as they chafed impatiently, under fire from the government cannon and awaiting the order to charge. Lochiel waited, too, sending messages asking that the order be given. When finally word came, the Camerons surged forward.

As these charging Jacobites bore down upon them, the government gunners changed their cannon ammunition from round-shot (cannonballs) to grapeshot (canvas bags filled with old metal, stones and any lethal rubbish the foragers could find). Cameron of Lochiel, claymore raised high, plunged onwards, leading his clansmen into that hail of artillery fire. Then he suddenly went down, as if felled, both ankles smashed by grapeshot. It was probably Sergeant Bristow's guns that did the damage; but his gun crew did not have long to celebrate, as their position was totally overwhelmed just seconds later.

From where Lochiel lay, he was able to see the initial success of the charge, as his Camerons tore into Barrell's Regiment. But then things changed for the worse, as devastating musket and mortar fire first slowed this Jacobite tide, then turned it.

As those that survived fled back across the moor, four of them raised up their wounded chief and carried him with them as they left the field. They quickly found a pony to mount him on and the time of 'skulking' in the heather began.

Lochiel, slowly healing, with the help of his brother, Doctor Archie, spent five months on the run. They were later joined by Prince Charles at Cluny MacPherson's refuge on Ben Alder and all three sailed for France on 19 September 1746.

Lochiel did not enjoy exile. Although Prince Charles secured him a position as colonel in Albany's Regiment he was restless. He saw another Jacobite rising as the only way to bring help to the clansmen he had left behind in Scotland and wrote on that theme to Prince Charles's Royal father.

One of Doctor Archie's hazardous return visits to the Highlands was in 1753. He had been sent regarding the retrieval or burial of the French gold which had been tardily landed at Borrodale in May 1746. While in the Highlands, he also carried out one of Lochiel's last wishes by sounding out feelings regarding another rising.

He was captured while secretly visiting David Stewart of Glenbuckie by soldiers from Inversnaid Barracks and taken to the Tower of London. It was said that he had been betrayed by the notorious Hanoverian spy 'Pickle'.

The government moved fast to protect their spy's identity. Doctor Archie was denied a fair trial and was instead judged on the seven-year-old Act of Attainder. This effectively condemned him, on the grounds of treason, to a death by hanging, drawing and quartering.

Although he was not permitted writing materials, the stub of a pencil was missed when he was searched. By this means, he was able to ignore his captors' edicts, and spent his last days writing a testament and also a letter to his son on carefully hoarded and precious scraps of paper.

The letter expressed concern for his ruined country and stated that, despite all the pressures brought to bear upon him by the Hanoverian government, he would never betray his friends. 'I should rather sacrifice my life than save it on dishonourable terms. I thank my God I was always easier ashamed than frightened,' he wrote.

So passed the man often referred to as the last Jacobite martyr, hanged at Tyburn on 7 June 1753. He was buried in the Savoy Chapel in London where, 240 years later, a brass plaque was dedicated to his memory, replacing two previous memorials destroyed by fire and war.

The Camerons that fell at Culloden are also commemorated, by a simpler memorial – their own rough stone – on the battlefield.

*The Clan Cameron Stone*

## Clan Mackintosh

Aeneas (Angus) Mackintosh was in his mid-30s when, succeeding his brother, he became the 22nd chief in 1740. He married the fiery 18-year-old Anne Farquharson of Invercauld the following year. She later helped him recruit the necessary men when he was commissioned as captain of one of the new Black Watch Companies in John Campbell, Earl of Loudon's Highlanders in December 1744.

The Farquharsons were a very pro-Jacobite clan, so there was no doubt in Anne's mind where her loyalties lay when Charles Edward Stuart landed in Scotland the following August. She must have been surprised when her husband seemed not to agree, and neither resigned his commission in King George's army nor raised his clan for the Prince.

However, Aeneas's duties with his Company often took him from home and this gave Anne ample opportunity to put her recruiting talents to work again, only this time for the Prince. She raised several hundred men of her husband's clan – and also from associated families, such as MacGillivray, MacBean, Shaw, etc. – to serve as the Jacobite Clan Chattan Regiment.

She placed her regiment under the command of Colonel Alexander MacGillivray of Dunmaglass and then watched them march south, while she remained at the clan seat, Moy Hall. The regiment joined the Prince's army in Perth in January 1746, going on to take part in the victory at the Battle of Falkirk.

Following this, the army returned to the north. Prince Charles reached Moy Hall ahead of the main force of his army on 16 February. He had a guard of only 30 men with him, and news of this soon reached Lord Loudon. Loudon was sure that by using decisive action at this point he could effectively end the 1745 rising. He hoped to capture Prince Charles, and so mobilised most of his force, about 1,500 men, and set out for Moy. But he had reckoned without any thought for the heroism and courage of a few remarkable individuals.

The Dowager Lady Mackintosh (Anne's mother-in-law) lived in Inverness and saw the preparations for the expedition. She sent Lachlan Mackintosh, who was about fifteen years of age, with a message to Moy, eight miles away, through the darkest night on foot. At first Lachlan could not get past Loudon's men but, with his local knowledge, he chose a different route, at his fastest run, and got to Moy at around five in the morning, shouting alarm to all who would listen and telling the household that an army of redcoats were only a mile away. One account describes Lady Anne as 'running around like a madwoman in her shift', before getting hold of herself and organising the Prince's safe evacuation, down the loch side, out of harm's way.

Meanwhile, the other heroes of that night were about to play their part. Much earlier, and by sheerest coincidence unconnected to Loudon's advance, Lady Anne had just through prudence deployed five men to watch the road to Inverness. Donald Fraser, the Moy blacksmith, was the captain of this guard. They saw the redcoat advance and let off some shots, killing Lord MacLeod's piper, Donald MacCrimmon – who had notoriously foretold his own death in his composition, 'MacCrimmon's Lament', just before leaving Skye.

The five scouts also shouted back and fore, making a good job of sounding like several clan regiments about to attack. Confounded by darkness, and fearful of an attack by a large force, Loudon panicked and retreated fast for Inverness. This became known as the Rout of Moy, and with good reason: five men putting fifteen hundred to flight!

The Jacobites entered Inverness on 18 February, also the day of Loudon's retreat north into Ross-shire. Men were deployed north to pursue him and following a successful military engagement near Dornoch on 20 March, Aeneas Mackintosh of Mackintosh (who had been with Loudon's forces) was captured. The Prince paroled this captain (company commander) into the hands of his wife (nominally a regimental commander), saying he 'could not be in better security, or more honourably treated'. She allegedly greeted Aeneas with the words, 'Your servant, captain', to which he replied, 'Your servant, colonel', so bestowing upon her that well-known title of 'Colonel Anne'.

A month later, her 350 men were standing, and dying, on the field of Culloden, near breaking, under continuous cannon fire, drifting smoke and the stench of sulphur. Finally, the order came – 'Claymore!' – and they were off, loping down the field, unable to hold back longer and determined to have vengeance for friends and relatives already lost.

Their regiment was one that suffered severely. They ran under a hail of mortar fire and into the face of lethal and well-drilled musket files, firing at the rate of three balls a minute. The terrible grapeshot ripped holes feet wide in their ranks and by the time they scythed through the government front line with a juddering crash, they were subject to the withering enfilade fire of Wolfe's Regiment and were falling many deep. They lost their colonel and, out of a full complement of twenty-one officers, only eight survivors are named.

As the last shots were fired, the dead of Clan Chattan lay so thick that when the time came to bury them they filled three different pits.

Eyewitnesses say that on 18 April a party of men was detached to put to death all wounded Jacobites in and about the field of battle. That same day, a further party of 200 men commanded by Colonel Cockayne was sent to bring in 'Colonel Anne'.

This party killed at least 14 men, women and children as they made their way to Moy, where they looted the house and hit Lady Mackintosh with gun butts. Rescued from further indignity by one Sir Everard Fawkner, she was then mounted on a pony and the drummers played the dead beat as the party left her house.

Although imprisoned in rooms in Inverness, she was well treated thereafter and was able to pass on some provisions to prisoners less well off than she. Release from custody came at the end of six weeks. Not only did she and Aeneas both survive the conflict, even more remarkably so did their marriage.

*The Clan Mackintosh Stone*

# Clan MacGillivray

The MacGillivrays are an ancient clan, said to have originated in Lochaber. There are accounts that suggest they sought the protection of Farquhar, 5th chief of Clan Mackintosh, as early as 1268. When the ensuing Mackintosh chief quit his Lochaber home and returned to Badenoch, the MacGillivrays followed them into the north-east, settling finally on the lands of Dunmaglass in Strathnairn.

The MacGillivrays remained loyal to Clan Chattan, and the Mackintoshes, for easily the next 500 years and this undoubtedly influenced Lady Anne Mackintosh in 1745. Despite being only in her very early 20s, we have heard how 'Colonel Anne' Mackintosh raised her husband's clan for the Prince. She obviously could not lead them on campaign, so needed a field commander for her regiment. The man she chose was Alexander MacGillivray of Dunmaglass: he had, after all, already seen foreign service and it is claimed was a respected leader and a fearless warrior, some 6 ft 5 in. tall.

His fiancée was the accomplished and beautiful Elizabeth Campbell of Clunas. Her father, Duncan, was a man of Jacobite sympathies who had been exiled after the 1715 rising. While living in Rome, he had married Catherine Trotter and in 1724 she had given birth to Elizabeth. The girl received her early education in the city, but when Catherine died unexpectedly Duncan felt prompted to return to Scotland, where he knew that his motherless daughter would benefit from having relatives around her.

Elizabeth grew up in Delnies, then later in Clunas. She was lauded and courted by many suitors but only had eyes for Alexander MacGillivray. He was quoted as being the fairest, handsomest youth in the Highlands, fine-featured and red-haired, which gave him his Gaelic name, 'Alistair-Ruadh-na Feile' (Red Alexander).

Tradition states that when the men of Clan Chattan gathered, before Culloden, they sharpened their swords on an ancient stone, the Clach an Airm (see Part Three). This seems likely, as Alexander lived nearby at the time, at Easter Gask.

Some accounts have Elizabeth approaching Drummossie Moor on the morning of 16 April, proud to see her man busy marshalling the 350 men of Clan Chattan.

As with Lady Mackintosh, Elizabeth's family too was divided by the troubles. While Duncan was a Jacobite, his own father, Sir Archibald Campbell, was a staunch Hanoverian; likewise Duncan's younger brother (Elizabeth's uncle Colin, a doctor in Inverness) was married to a sister of Duncan Forbes of Culloden, Lord President and a prominent Hanoverian.

Alexander led Clan Chattan heroically on the field at Culloden. His regiment was the first to charge and he found himself amidst the heaviest hand-to-hand fighting. He broke through the government front line, striking down many foes as he passed. But with momentum gone before he hit the second line and suffering severe wounds, he fell, crawling towards a well. There he died, with many of his clan: the water ran red in the spring thereafter called 'the Well of the Dead'.

After the battle, his body was seen by a local woman, who tied a handkerchief to his arm so that Elizabeth might recognise him on that moor amidst so many dead.

Records state:

> After the battle, his body with fifty others was thrown into a large pit, and so far did the King's troops carry their animosity, that for six weeks they guarded the field and would not grant the poor consolation . . . of placing these mangled carcases in their family burying places. However, at the end of that time, the relations of Dunmaglass dug up the pit . . . The place they had been thrown into being a moss, is supposed to be the cause of the corpse remaining uncorrupted.

Elizabeth was able to help to arrange for him to be taken to Petty church, where he was allegedly re-interred secretly, under the doorstep. Elizabeth's own grave can be found at the lonely ruined chapel of Barevan. The inscription reads:

> Under this stone are interred the remains of Duncan Campbell of Clunese, and Elizabeth, his only child by Catherine, daughter of John Trotter of Morton Hall, Esq. He died, 23rd January, 1766, aged seventy-five, and she, 22nd August, 1746, aged twenty-four. D.C.E.C.

She survived the death of her betrothed by only about four months, long enough to ensure his interment in consecrated ground, after which, stricken, she died of a broken heart.

*The stone for Alexander of Dunmaglass (Alistair-Ruadh-na-Feile),
the chief of the MacGillivrays*

# Atholl Highlanders

Atholl is a potent name in Scottish history. It is one of the houses from which the Scottish King was traditionally drawn. Blair Castle, standing in the Vale of Atholl, is home to the Dukes of that line. At the time of the 1715 rising, the Duke remained loyal to the Whig establishment and the Hanoverian succession, as did one of his younger sons, James. Meanwhile William, Marquis of Tullibardine, the Duke's heir, raised four regiments for the Jacobites and was joined by two of his other brothers, Lords George and Charles Murray.

By the time of the '45 rising, therefore, both James and William were known as the Duke of Atholl – the younger brother recognised by the Whig establishment, the elder by the Jacobites. William, the Jacobite Duke, raised the Atholl Brigade, comprising three battalions, for Prince Charles. These 'Atholl Highlanders' included large numbers of Robertsons, Reids, Perthshire Stewarts, Menzies, Murrays and MacGregors. There was also a significant contingent of Campbells from Glenlyon, under Archibald Roy, son to Glenlyon himself. Lord George Murray, Duke William's younger brother, was both the battalion commander and a lieutenant general of the whole Jacobite army.

The Atholl Brigade fought at Prestonpans and was also part of the force which marched south through England. Lord George began to lose Prince Charles's favour at Carlisle and this was compounded at Derby, when he spoke in favour of a retreat northwards. The brigade took part in the Battle of Falkirk and was active during March in a campaign against Hanoverian outposts in Perthshire. They were recalled to Inverness in April as a forthcoming clash between Prince Charles and the Duke of Cumberland was being anticipated.

Cumberland's troops poured out of Aberdeen on 8 April, heading west. The Jacobite intention was to attack the government army as it crossed the River Spey. The river was running 'belly-deep' and the footing was unsteady. However, this plan came to nothing, due to the speed of Cumberland's march and his choice of an unexpected crossing point. The Jacobites were caught totally unprepared and, lacking enough regiments, could provide only token resistance to the crossing. Lord Elcho's Lifeguards were there, and some shots were exchanged, but even this was fraught with irony. Captain David Hunter, in the heat of the moment, was less than careful when firing his pistol at the enemy: he foolishly wounded his own horse in the neck and the unfortunate beast, understandably distressed, threw him. Just at the moment when his capture appeared unavoidable, one of his companions galloped in, swung David up behind him and the two of them won clear.

Yet the Spey was lost, and so now ground had to be chosen for the coming confrontation. A view prevailed, in Jacobite council, that Inverness must be protected at all costs, due to its importance as a supply port and because its warehouses contained all the Jacobite stores. This led to the decision to make a stand on Drummossie Moor.

Lord George Murray was deeply unhappy with the choice of ground but was unable to persuade the Prince otherwise. The Atholl Brigade was placed on the Jacobite right and when they charged, Lord George was in the thickest of the action with them. Even when everything came apart, he was one of the last to leave the fray. Hatless, wigless and brandishing his notched and battered sword, he finally saw that all was lost and his place was to command the remnant of his brigade on their retreat from the field. He led his men to the muster at Ruthven, in Badenoch, the next day, where they dispersed thereafter. Lord George escaped to Holland in December 1746 and was well received in Rome by the Prince's father. He went on to live in numerous places on the Continent and died in Holland in 1760, at the age of 66.

## Clan MacLachlan

The clan seat of the MacLachlans is Castle Lachlan, on the western side of Loch Fyne, in Argyllshire. The 17th chief, Lachlan, led about 150 men to join the Prince in Edinburgh in September 1745. He had hoped to raise a larger force, but the MacLachan lands were closely interwoven with those of that leading Hanoverian the Duke of Argyll.

The MacLachlans fought in the second line at Prestonpans and then marched with the army to Carlisle. There, the Prince arranged for 30 of the MacLachans to join the Atholl Brigade for the march into England. Lachlan was sent back to Perth, with the remainder of his troops and 16 cavalrymen. His commission, given by Prince Charles, was to lead the 3,000 men that were waiting in Perth south into England.

It is alleged that this endeavour failed because, although the men were willing to embark upon such a foreign adventure, Lord Strathallan, then governor of Perth, refused to comply.

Perhaps Strathallan was shrewd enough to sense how the following few weeks might unfold and that these new levies would not appreciably alter any decisions the commanders in the south would have to take. The Jacobites were back in Scotland by late December, and MacLachlan and his men rejoined them in Stirling, in time for the Battle of Falkirk. Prince Charles also appointed the MacLachlan chief as commissary general for the army.

One aide-de-camp was another Lachlan MacLachlan. He was the son of the chief and the man chosen to take the Culloden order to charge – 'Claymore!' – along the line. Young MacLachlan being decapitated by a cannonball before delivering this order did nothing for either Jacobite morale or combat organisation.

After it was realised that communications had been so brutally cut, a second messenger was sent. This was Colonel Harry Ker of Graden. It was on receiving his word that the front line surged into action.

At Culloden, the chief of MacLachlan's command, at the rank of colonel, was the joint regiment of MacLeans and MacLachlans. This regiment stood on the front line, between Clan Chattan and the Stewarts of Appin. It is said that the colonel was the last man to receive direct orders from the Prince on the field of battle. Following this, he rode swiftly back to his regiment to lead them upon the enemy. His death, sudden and unexpected, came some minutes later, an eyewitness describing it as follows: 'The Laird of MacLachlan had his abdomen laid on his horse neck by a cannon bullet.'

# Clan MacLean

The MacLeans had been out as Jacobites in the 1715, and this was one reason why Sir Hector MacLean of Duart was arrested by the government on suspicion as early as June 1745. It therefore fell to Charles MacLean of Drimnin to lead Clan MacLean in the '45 rising, aided by his three sons as captains. As well as his Morvern men, there were also some of Duart's MacLeans and some Ardgour MacLeans. Drimnin was given the title of lieutenant colonel of the combined regiment, making him MacLachlan's second in command. When the colonel fell, MacLean took over, finishing the charge across the field.

By the time the retreat began, most of his men had been killed and Allan, his son, told him that his other two sons had fallen. Turning back into the carnage, he cried, 'It shall not be for nought!' Two of Cobham's dragoons rode at him. He killed one and wounded the other but was then attacked by more troopers, who cut him to pieces.

Of nine-score men that MacLean of Drimnin took out on the rising, it is said that only thirty-eight made it home again. Most of the rest lie near the MacLean Stone.

*The stone for MacGillivray, MacLean,*
*MacLachlan and Atholl Highlanders*

# The Edinburgh Regiment and John Roy Stewart

The Edinburgh Regiment comprised a curious mixture of recruits from the backstreets and closes of Edinburgh, deserters from the government army defeated at Prestonpans and 50 or so Strathbraan men transferred from the Atholl Brigade by Lord George Murray.

They were raised by John Roy Stewart, one of the most colourful of Bonnie Prince Charlie's supporters. Born in 1700, in Kincardine, in Strathspey, his early education was good and was culturally augmented by residence in both France and Portugal. He was both a writer of poetry and of songs. He joined the British Army, and was both lieutenant, and quartermaster with the Scots Greys. He had high hopes of a commission in the Black Watch, which was recruiting in 1730. This came to nothing, however, and, with the ashes of disappointment in his mouth, he left the army and began the business of Jacobite politicking and plotting.

He went to France in the late 1730s and was active in fighting against his former regiment in Flanders, particularly at the famous French victory of Fontenoy in May 1745.

When news of Prince Charles's campaign reached him, he travelled immediately to join the rising, meeting the Prince at Blair Atholl. Charles was delighted with this adventurer and professional soldier. Two weeks later, the Battle of Prestonpans had been won and the Edinburgh Regiment was being formed. This was not so difficult for John Roy, who had been stationed in Edinburgh during his time with the Scots Greys. There were also men from his native Strathspey within the ranks. The regiment took part in the march to Derby, the Battles of Clifton and Falkirk, and then the move north through the Highlands. At that time, in particular, many of the orders related to John Roy's Regiment being used for patrolling and scouting.

The Edinburgh Regiment was about 200 strong at the Battle of Culloden. It was in the Jacobite front line and suffered heavy casualties. After the defeat, John Roy seems first to have gone to Gorthleck and then onwards to the gathering at Ruthven.

He was also at the final gathering of Jacobite leaders at Murlaggan on Loch Arkaig in May. There, he discussed with Lochiel, Ardsheal, Cluny and others the possibilities of raising more men and keeping the rising alive. Their plans bore little fruit, however, and it was accepted that to continue without significant French support was impossible. They chose, instead, to scatter, each to seek his own refuge until escape was possible.

John Roy headed for the familiar hills of Strathspey. This was his home country and the local folk never betrayed him, despite the offer of a large reward. His songs and writings place him, at various times, nursing a sprained foot under the waterfall of Slugan-an-Eas, narrowly evading capture in Glenmore and in a cave on the hill of Craiggowrie, from which he could survey all the surrounding countryside.

Latterly, he moved slightly farther north, near to Nethybridge. It is said that he attended a wedding in Balnagown, dancing merrily into the night. His next refuge was Bad-an-Aodinn (Badenedin), where he was almost caught. A local girl, Mary Grant, just managed to warn him in time that redcoats were on their way. He wrapped a ragged old plaid about him and, taking a staff, played a very convincing old, lame beggar. In this way, he hobbled painfully into the shelter of the nearest forest, where he threw down his disguise, then ran off, as fast as his miraculously healed legs would carry him. His friend, John Stewart, lived at Connage, across the hill. John Roy was hiding in the gorge below this farm when word came that Cluny MacPherson wished to meet with him at Ben Alder.

John Roy packed his meagre belongings without delay and set off, southwards through Badenoch, joining Cluny below Ben Alder on 13 September. There, he was surprised and delighted to discover that the Prince was already with Cluny, together with Lochiel and others. There was news of French ships lying off the west coast, and so John Roy joined the Prince's party on what would be their last Highland journey.

They arrived at Borrodale on 19 September, where Cluny bid them farewell before their ship slipped out of Loch nan Uamh, bearing them safely to France.

John Roy Stewart never returned to Scotland and died six years later, in 1752. He did, however, leave us a legacy of both verse and song. One of the most enduring of these is a parody of the 23rd psalm which brims with rough good humour and rugged self-confidence.

> The Lord's my targe, I will be stout,
> With dirk and trusty blade,
> Though Campbells come in flocks about
> I will not be afraid.
>
> The Lord's the same as heretofore,
> He's always good to me;
> Though red-coats come a thousand more,
> Afraid I will not be.
>
> Though they the woods do cut and burn,
> And drain the lochs all dry;
> Though they the rocks do overturn
> And change the course of Spey;
>
> Though they mow down both corn and grass,
> Nay seek me underground;
> Though hundreds guard each road and pass –
> John Roy will not be found.

# Clan Campbell

Clan Campbell was amongst the most powerful of the Highland clans in the eighteenth century. This did not, however, protect them from the internal divisions seen everywhere in this civil war.

The Campbells of Argyll, Loudon and Breadalbane all declared for the House of Hanover and provided men for the Argyll Militia. Meanwhile Campbell of Glenlyon raised his men for the Jacobites, both in 1715 and 1745.

In the '45 rising, Glenlyon's son, Archibald Roy, brought these Campbells to the Atholl Brigade. The reasons for Glenlyon's pro-Jacobite stance probably included the fact that his lands were long miles distant from Clan Campbell's centre of power in Argyll and that the Glenlyon Campbells moved in different circles, being related by marriage to the fiercely Jacobite MacGregors of Glengyle. Glenlyon was, in fact, Rob Roy's cousin.

On the day of the Battle of Culloden, the Argyll Militia was commanded by John Campbell (Colonel Jack), son of Campbell of Mamore. The militia had been used as scouting patrols since first light and, as the government army formed up ready for battle, they were ordered to move to the rear to guard the baggage. Four companies on the far left never received – or chose to ignore – this order to fall back. These companies were commanded by Captain Colin Campbell of Ballimore; they achieved fame as the infantry that broke down the walls of the Culwhiniac enclosure. This allowed the dragoons to begin their outflanking manoeuvre to the south.

Ballimore's companies moved uphill and became locked in a firefight with the Royal Ecossais over the stone walls of the enclosure. Ballimore was shot down while crossing a gap in the wall, but most of the eight Campbells lost in this engagement were 'head-shot' (a consequence of their position, in cover, behind the wall).

The fallen of Ballimore's companies are commemorated in the Campbell Stone, although it could probably be seen as a suitable marker for any Glenlyons, too. They fought on the extreme right of the Jacobite line and so their casualties would also have fallen in this general area.

There was reconciliation within Clan Campbell after the '45. Archibald, third Duke of Argyll, was a fierce opponent of Jacobitism generally and his later harsh treatment of 'James of the Glen' shows an unflinching absolutism; however, he both called for, and practised, leniency towards Campbell Jacobites. He even went as far as to have new charters made out to those of his vassals who had supported the House of Stuart, saying that he wished to do to others as he would be done by.

*The Campbell Stone*

## The Stewarts of Appin

The green and wooded lands lying along the eastern shores of the Firth of Lorn are known as Appin. They had long been ancestral clanlands of the Stewarts, who had been 'out' in every rising since Dundee's attempt back in 1689. The '45 was to be no different, although in this case their chief, Dougal Stewart, refused to become involved; he was generally considered a drunk and a spendthrift. The task of leadership, therefore, fell to his uncle, Charles Stewart of Ardsheal – tutor, expert swordsman and Jacobite of long-standing.

At Culloden, the regiment comprised about 300 men, some of whom were later to become immortalised in literature, while others went on to sire famous descendants.

Malcolm, the great-grandfather of the famous missionary, Dr David Livingstone, was there, as was Captain Donald Dubh MacLaren of Invernentie. Donald Dubh was leading his clansmen from the Braes of Balquidder and in his hand was clasped the fearsome Invernentie Sword.

Captain Alexander Stewart of Invernahyle was present and would be wounded in the course of the battle. He survived and became famous in later years due to his association with Sir Walter Scott. In fact Scott comments, in the letter quoted in this book's introduction:

> My father, although a Borderer, transacted business for
> many Highland lairds, and particularly for one old man
> called Stewart of Invernahyle, who had been out both in
> 1715 and '45, and whose tales were the absolute delight
> of my childhood.

Another storyteller, Robert Louis Stevenson, wove his tales *Kidnapped* and *Catriona* around two other members of the Appin Regiment – Captain James Stewart (James of the Glen) and his foster son, Alan Breac Stewart.

Alan Breac did not begin the '45 within the Jacobite army, however. Some time prior to these stirring times, he had, like many others in Scotland, chosen to take the King's shilling. He had enlisted in the Essex Regiment and fought with them at the Battle of Prestonpans. It was on that field, after the conflict ended, that he deserted from his regiment and joined the Appin Regiment.

After Culloden, he escaped to France, later returning to visit his foster father in 1752, while on an illegal recruiting drive for Ogilvy's Regiment in the French Service. It was during this trip that notorious events unfolded which are still hotly debated to this day.

By 1752, James of the Glen had been pardoned and was living at Acharn, back in Appin. The government factor locally was Colin Campbell of Glenure (sometimes called Red Colin, and immortalised by Robert Louis Stevenson as the Red Fox). Tensions were running high in both Appin and Lochaber that year over issues of rent collections and impending evictions.

Late in the day, on 14 May, a single shot echoed in the shadows of the wood of Lettermore. Red Colin was left dying on the track through the wood; his killer, only glimpsed through thick undergrowth, got clean away.

The assassin was generally assumed to be Alan Breac, and he certainly left the country in a hurry. He was last seen near Kinlochrannoch on 20 May and never returned thereafter.

The man that was left to pay the price was his foster father, James. Almost certainly wholly innocent, he was made a convenient scapegoat. He was tried in September, with perjured evidence ensuring he was found guilty of being accomplice to the murder. He was hanged at Ballachulish on 8 November – by a regime still consumed by the need to make such examples of those they deemed rebels.

The Duke of Argyll required that poor James's bones be wired and left hanging, and so they did, for three long years. But love and respect for him in local hearts has outlasted that barbaric and unjust sentence by centuries.

However the murder of the Red Fox was still many years in the future on the day in 1746 when the men of Appin stood on Drummossie Moor, beneath their standard snapping in the strong easterly wind. That yellow Saltire upon the blue silk meant everything to them. The colours seemed particularly vivid when seen against the dark sleet-filled sky, and those men felt that their honour was contained within that brave banner.

'Claymore!' came the call to charge. Running, volleys, shouting, cannon-smoke and musket-smoke, sulphur-stenching heavy in the air – disaster and retreat.

Almost half of the regiment are dead or wounded. And then, the unthinkable. The colours are down. Another lifts that sacred banner, only to die in a welter of blood and bone. Then another takes the flag, and falls, followed by over a dozen desperate men, each trying to salvage the honour of the regiment.

The colours were finally rescued by Donald Livingstone (Domhnull Molach), who, turning back, under fire, took the banner from the pole and wrapped it around his body. Donald, a lad of only about 18 years, took the banner safely back to Appin, so saving it from the fate of many of the colours that were captured that day.

*The Clan Stewart of Appin Stone*

Fourteen of the Jacobite banners were burned by the public hangman in the Grassmarket in Edinburgh in June 1746, and one was burned in Glasgow, signalling an end to military Jacobitism in Britain. Some other banners, however, just like that of the Appin Regiment, were saved and took on the mantle of legend.

Clan Chattan's banner was saved by a young man from Flemington. Ever after he was called Domhnull na Braiteach, Donald of the Colours. This by-name was even passed on to his sons, who became known throughout their lives as Angus and Charles of the Colours.

MacPherson's banner was saved by virtue of it not having been present on the field – Cluny MacPherson's Regiment were unable to reach the field of battle in time. They began meeting the survivors at Dalmagarry, near Moy.

The Cameron colours were saved and can be seen at Achnacarry Castle. The bearer was traditionally MacLachlan of Coruanan, on Loch Linnhe, just south of Fort William.

John Roy Stewart's banner from the Edinburgh Regiment is said to have been taken from the field by one James MacIntyre, who faithfully flew it at the top of the Cairngorms every year for the next 40, on the anniversary of the raising of the standard at Glenfinnan.

Ogilvy's Forfarshire Regiment was still an orderly military unit as it left the field. They protected their regimental standard as they travelled south, leaving it for safekeeping in a house in Kirriemuir. It made its way into Dundee's museum in the twentieth century.

Two other banners that were rumoured to have been saved were those of the Duke of Perth and Lord Balmerino's troop of the Lifeguards.

The survival of these banners was, for the Jacobites, like the survival of a tiny light in their darkness – a promise of hope, and a scrap of pride.

## The French and Irish Regiments

It was a dark night on 20 March 1746. The men were doing their best to stay quiet as they circled the town of Keith. Major Nicholas Glasgow had come up with the brilliant plan of entering the town from the south-east to engage the Argyll Militia while masquerading as Hanoverian forces. The attack was a complete success and, with the loss of only one man, he and his men killed nine of the enemy and took eighty prisoners and thirty horses. So where had this wily strategist come from?

Nicholas Glasgow had been a lieutenant in Dillon's French–Irish Regiment and was appointed major and military instructor to Lord Ogilvy's second battalion. Lord John Drummond had brought French Service troops to Scotland as part of the French assistance promised by Louis of France (see New Lands, New Challenges, Part Three). They were drawn from his own French regiment and also from each of the six Irish Regiments comprising Louis XV's Irish Brigade. They landed at Montrose on 24 and 26 November.

These French–Irish Regiments stood firm at Culloden as the defeat unfolded. They fired repeated volleys at dragoons in pursuit of fleeing Jacobites and hence covered the retreat. They lost almost half their number and their commanding officer in this gallant action. On surrendering, however, they were at least treated as prisoners of war, unlike the Scottish and English Jacobites, who were deemed to be treasonous rebels to be hunted down and killed.

Major Glasgow was also captured at Culloden and was sent to London for trial. He pleaded that he was born in France and held a French commission. The court recognised this and he was later discharged and returned to France.

In the years since the battle, both a French Stone and an Irish Stone have been erected on the field in memory of the men of these regiments who fell and their selfless defence of their allies on 16 April 1746.

The tale of Major Glasgow is recounted in the trilogy entitled *Prisoners of the '45*, published by the Scottish History Society. There are a great many other tales within the pages of those books, many of which are often told at Culloden and deserve to be told here.

The ships that managed to reach Montrose were only a portion of Drummond's fleet. Other ships, laden with men and arms, were also bound for Montrose in that final week in November. The British Navy blockade was proving effective, however, intercepting ships like *Louis XV* and imprisoning the troops aboard. Throughout the rising, close to a thousand French troops were captured at sea. Alexander Baillie, a captain in the French Service, was aboard *L'Esperance* when she was captured on 25 November. He was transferred to a custom-house vessel at Greenwich until his pardon (on condition of perpetual banishment) in July 1747.

Ignatius Brown, described as a French Irishman, with Lally's Regiment in the French Service, came to Scotland earlier, with the French envoy in October 1745. He was appointed colonel by the Prince and was left as part of the force expected to hold Carlisle when the Jacobite army retired northwards. He escaped during the fall of Carlisle and rejoined the Prince in time to fight in the Battle of Falkirk. Charles then sent him to France to inform Louis XV of the victory, after which he returned, leading some fresh French troops, in March 1746. This was aboard *Prince Charles* (known as *Hazard* until November 1745), captained by George Talbot. Their ship was driven ashore at Tongue by four British Navy warships and those on board were taken prisoner by Lord Reay and his militia. Ignatius was sent to London as a French prisoner of war and later pardoned – on the same day, and under the same conditions, as Alexander Baillie.

Some people ashore were also imprisoned, due to involvement in importation of French arms. Robert Mitchell, a brewer from Johnshaven, assisted with provisioning the French ships at Stonehaven and supplying the French officers with horses. He had assisted in the plunder of the *Hazard* upon her original capture by Nicholas Glasgow in Montrose and also captured two government spies in the same area. It is said that he was in charge of the landing of fourteen boatloads of ammunition, by bonfire light, at Johnshaven, and perhaps his most colourful moment came as he was leaving his neighbourhood fully armed. He was asked by some of the locals what he was planning. His answer, with a laugh, was that he was off to shoot the Duke of Cumberland. With that, he joined Bannerman's Company and went on to fight at Culloden. However, his ambition for Cumberland came to nothing and, by May, Robert was a prisoner. He was last heard of at Tilbury Fort and may well have died there.

The preceding suite of story fragments all relate to prisoners with a connection to the French and Irish Regiments. There are also, of course, a range of tales about the other prisoners, some humorous, some stirring and some downright tragic, and these are included in the following section, entitled 'Prisoners'.

# Prisoners

About 3,500 people were imprisoned by the government before, during and after the 1745 rising. Their records, in some part, tell their stories and present a picture of men, women and children locked up, sometimes for months, or even years, on suspicion of a number of alleged crimes.

Many of these people died, or were transported overseas, for charges ranging from being in arms with the Jacobite forces right through to just not being helpful enough with the redcoat patrols. Including camp followers, they ranged in age from babes in arms to octogenarians, although active soldiers were generally between 14 and 70 years of age.

John Auld was a 14 year old from Falkirk. He was captured after Culloden, where he had served as a drummer to Kilmarnock's Horse Grenadiers. After being imprisoned in Stirling, Edinburgh and Carlisle, he was eventually transported to the Americas, despite testifying that his stepfather had forced him to serve.

Alexander Bowar of Meathie was abroad when the Prince landed. Loyal to the House of Stuart, he hurried home, raised his tenants and joined Ogilvy's Regiment as a lieutenant. After the Battle of Culloden, he returned home, in hiding, but was soon discovered by a party of dragoons. He put up a good fight but was captured and taken to Perth. His wife went at once to Stirling Castle, seeking mercy from the Duke of Cumberland. She must have been convincing, as the Duke agreed to save Alexander's life in return for their undertaking to leave the country and never return. Having received safe passes for the entire family, the lady then travelled quickly back to Perth – only to find that Alexander had died in prison due to the wounds he had received as he was captured. This irony was just too much for her to bear: when she was shown his body, she fell dead on the spot.

Young Alexander Buchanan's story is very different. From Auchleishie in Perthshire, this 19 year old became a captain in the Duke of Perth's Regiment. He was captured in June 1746 and was kept on one of the prison ships on the Thames until his trial in November. Happily for Alexander, he was acquitted on the grounds of his youth and on evidence that he had been forced to serve. Not so happily, however, he somehow got lost in the system and was transported by mistake to Maryland in February 1747, probably on the ship the *Gildart*.

Stewart Carmichael of Bonnyhaugh was more than once a prisoner. He was first captured as one of Reverend Robert Forbes's party on their way north to join the Prince in September 1745. He is said to have escaped early in 1746 but is recorded as being recaptured in Orkney, in May, and taken to London. He was imprisoned on the prison ship HMS *Pamela* at Tilbury but escaped in September by jumping into the Thames, with some bladders for flotation. Paddling ashore, he then hid in London until the publication of general indemnity made it safe to break cover.

John Cattanach was valet to Captain William Ogilvy, of Ogilvy's Regiment. They both fought at Culloden and after the defeat returned home. John was taken prisoner at Cortachy during June, but was soon released; however, he did then become a frequent visitor at the enemy headquarters. This led to the suspicion that he had become an informer and he was subsequently murdered by some of his former comrades.

Robert Forbes, from Strathbogie, was a tenant to the Duke of Gordon. He was a captain in Lord Lewis Gordon's Regiment and was taken at the fall of Carlisle. At his trial in London the following October, it was proved that he had been forced to serve, that he had previously shown Hanoverian sympathies by providing hay for General Cope's army and also that, while at Carlisle, he had tried to escape over the walls in women's clothing but was stopped. He was understandably acquitted.

The outcome was darker for Charles Gordon, from Terpersie in Aberdeenshire. He was a volunteer with Gordon of Glenbucket's Regiment. It was months after Culloden that he was captured in his own house in the north-east of Scotland. The troopers did not know who they had caught and took him to a neighbouring farmhouse. This was where his family had been sheltering, however, and when his children saw him they called out 'Daddy'. He was taken to Carlisle, pleaded guilty at his trial and was executed there in mid-November.

Peter McConachy was not even a Jacobite. He was a Hanoverian schoolmaster from Glass, near Huntly. He had heard a rumour that John Roy Stewart was likely to attempt another surprise attack, following Major Glasgow's success at Keith, and reported this to Lord Albemarle, who consequently put the troops on alert for several nights. There was no attack, and Albemarle assumed McConachy's report to be mere harassment, so had him arrested. He was convicted of 'spreading false intelligence'. He was sentenced to be 'whipped and drum'd through . . . Aberdeen, Old Meldrum and Strathbogey', and then 'turned towards the rebels with orders never to come near where the army may be, on pain of being Hanged'.

When everything went bad on the field of Culloden, the leader of the MacLarens cut his way clear of the conflict. As previously mentioned, he was Donald MacLaren of Invernentie, in Balquidder. He was later captured on 19 July at a hut on the Braes of Leny, sustaining a thigh wound in the process. He was, thereafter, strapped to a dragoon to keep him under control during his journey to prison in Carlisle. Getting hold of a blade, however, he chose his moment, cut the strap and threw himself over a cliff to escape. This place, on Erickstane Brae, is still called 'MacLaren's Leap'. Following this audacious escape, he returned to his own area, where he remained – in hiding and in disguise – until the Act of Indemnity.

Walter Mitchell was only 17 and a student at Aberdeen University when he went to Buchan to avoid being forced out by Glenbucket's men. Ironically, Pitsligo's men found him and forced him into the army. His mother, an ale-house keeper, offered to give them money in place of her son, but they refused, saying it was men they needed. He was given the position of ensign with the Duke of Perth's Regiment and was captured at Carlisle. He was sentenced to death in October, but his mother pleaded that she had supplied General Cope with both hay and straw at Banff. This information led to a reprieve and, in September 1748, his sentence was commuted to banishment to America.

James Reid was a piper from Angus who served with Ogilvy's Regiment. He was taken during the capture of Carlisle. His trial was held the following October in York, where it was pointed out that he was only a piper and so was recommended for mercy. Yet the court still found him guilty in a landmark ruling on the bagpipes. *Prisoners of the '45* relates that it was judged that 'no regiment ever marched without musical instruments such as drums, trumpets and the like; and that a Highland regiment never marched without a piper, therefore his bagpipe, in the eye of the law, was an instrument of war'. As a result, James Reid was executed at York on 15 November 1746.

The Reverend William Seton was an Episcopal minister from

Forfar. He was imprisoned in May 1746 for preaching a rebellious sermon from Jeremiah, 8.4: 'Thus saith the Lord; Shall they fall, and not arise? Shall he turn away and not return?'

Reverend Seton was discharged from Montrose jail on 28 August of that same year.

These dozen tales are but the smallest portion of the prisoners' stories. Every prisoner – Jacobite or Hanoverian – had their own tale and each was as worthy as the next. These few pages could be seen as standing witness for all the untold stories.

## Clan Chisholm

The Chisholms may have been a Norman family, attracted to the Scottish Borders by David I's policies. The first Chisholm recorded as living in the Highlands was Sir Robert Chisholm, in the mid-fourteenth century. He succeeded to the positions of Justiciar, Constable of Urquhart Castle and Sheriff of Inverness. An advantageous marriage later secured the family the lands of Cannich and Strathglass, and the leadership of a Highland clan who took the Chisholm name.

Roderick Chisholm, said to have been born 1688–9, became chief around 1708. He married Elizabeth, the daughter of MacDonell of Glengarry, in 1713 and later raised 200 men to fight for the Jacobites in the 1715 rising. Proscription and land forfeiture followed the defeat at Sheriffmuir. Roderick was eventually pardoned in 1727 but was barred from regaining his estate (which was allowed, however, to pass to his eldest son, Alexander, in 1743).

By 1745, Roderick considered himself too old to lead men in a winter campaign. He persuaded Alexander, his eldest, to stay home and adopt a 'wait and see' strategy. His sons, John and James, were already serving officers in the British Army, so it was the youngest of his five boys, Roderick, who raised the clan that December for Prince Charles. This was probably with his father's consent, as Chisholm was not one of those chiefs who later protested that their clan was raised against their wishes.

Clan Chisholm, acting with the Frasers, was busy that winter attacking Lord Loudon's forces in the north. The Chisholms then joined the main Jacobite army, sometime before April (possibly at Stirling, in February). By the morning of 16 April, young Roderick was standing on Drummossie Moor at the head of about 80 of his clansmen.

Sometime later, as the Duke of Cumberland's army tramped onto that same field, Lieutenants John and James Chisholm took up position with their regiment, known as Campbell's (the 21st of Foot), a bare half-mile from their youngest brother.

When the cannonade began, Roderick was one of the earliest casualties. Hit almost immediately by round-shot, he was being helped by some of his men when another ball struck, killing him outright. The Chisholms, therefore, had to charge without their colonel and at least 30 were to fall on the moor, near Campbell's Regiment, that day.

It is said that John and James later found their brother's body, which they laid out in some semblance of dignity, and then stood guard over it to ensure that it was safe from the atrocities unfolding all across the rest of the field.

It was undoubtedly a bleak time for these brothers, but things were to get no easier. In the aftermath of the battle, a terrible price was paid by many communities across the Highlands. One of the most notorious of the army commanders responsible for bringing fire, terror, rape, pillage and murder to these glens was Major W. Alexander Lockhart, a Lowland Scot and the Inverness commander. He was also the man who received a message about a redcoat trooper killed on the borders of Strathglass.

He ordered the Chisholms to ready a force to burn and harry their own lands and people the following day. Nothing the brothers could say would dissuade him. It was then John discovered that family loyalty is sometimes stronger than politics or army orders. He sent for his father's best hunter and got a room for him opposite Major Lockhart's quarters, near where today's Gellions Hotel stands on Bridge Street. That night, when Lockhart lit his lamp, one shot rang out, and he never lit another.

This vicious and sadistic officer seemed, by then, to be such an embarrassment to his superiors that on his death they took no punitive action against either John or the Chisholms, so Strathglass was quieter when the Prince hid there in August 1746.

One other (lesser-known) Chisholm tale was recently accessed at the National Archives of Scotland. It was written by Joseph Chisholm of Inverness in 1890 and originates in a tale told by his grandfather, who was Elder of Kilmorack Parish Church for 35 years and is the young son, of 16 years, referred to in the story.

> William Chisholm, my great-Grandfather, was a man of extraordinary bodily strength and activity. As soon as he heard that the Clan was to join the Prince, he placed himself under the Banner of his young Chief. They left their happy homes in the best of spirits, many of them to return no more. They marched into Inverness down the old road by the side of Craig Phadrig, and encamped for the night at the west side of the town, at Ballifeary, on land belonging to the Hon. M.P. for the County of Inverness, Charles Fraser Mackintosh.
>
> They joined the Prince's army next day, and went with it on the disastrous march to Nairn. On Drummossie Moor they were in the thickest of the fight when their young chief fell. When all was lost the few survivors retreated, my great-Grandfather being one of the few that escaped, and carried his trusty Claymore into Inverness. On the road, he was attacked by some dragoons, but he kept them at bay until some Highlanders came up, who soon made short work of them.

My great-Grandfather used to tell that the road from Culloden to Inverness was strewed with the dead bodies of our brave Highlanders. When he entered the town and made for the old bridge, he found that the enemy had it guarded to prevent any of the Highlanders retreating by that road. Seeing that there was no escape by that way, he made for the lower part of the town, and swam across the Ness. He arrived home safe, and told his friends how matters stood. They came to the conclusion that it would be best for him to make for a safe retreat and take his young son with him, as they were sure that the redcoats would be upon them at once.

Sure enough, the enemy Bloodhounds were all over the country the next day. A party of them called at my great-Grandmother's house and asked her where was her husband. She told them, very coolly, that he was on the hills looking after some cattle. Asked if he was at Culloden, she answered them that she knew nothing of Culloden. Singular to say, two of the party spoke Gaelic, which makes one think they were of the Campbells of Argyll. They made her then yoke a young black horse in a Loban [a peat cart], and walked it off, along with some more cattle they stole from some other Crofters. They went to Castle Downie, which they pillaged and then set fire to, and they threw the horse, Loban and all, into the blazing pile. He, being a spirited animal in the harness of a weak and primitive contraption, soon broke loose and escaped the fate intended for him.

About twelve midnight that same night he reached his home, and stood at the door neighing. My great-Grandmother rose to look out, and to her horror what did she think she saw but the ghost of her black horse. Her first exclamation was '*Mhaitheas bi mun cuairt orm, – Tannasg an Each dhubh againn!*' (Or in English, 'Goodness be about me, the Ghost of our black horse!'). And sure enough it was ghost-like, for the singeing and ashes that it got at Castle Downie changed its black coat for a greyish white.

When at last she ventured out she found that it was no ghost, but the real animal. She went over to him and found that he was suffering great pain from the scorching that he got in the flames of the castle. It was fortunate for the poor animal that there was some cream in the house that the redcoats missed, and she immediately brought it out and rubbed him all over with it and he seemed to get easier. She contrived to rub him every day for some weeks, until he was all right again, and he lived and worked on the Croft for seven years longer.

# Clan Fraser

Simon Fraser (MacShimi in Gaelic being 'son of Simon') was the 11th Lord Lovat. Castle Dounie (now replaced by Beaufort), near Beauly, was his seat and, from there, he politicked all through the Jacobite period.

He initially supported William and Mary, only to betray them in 1689 by taking the Jacobite part. He fled to France but was back in Britain as Whig and Hanoverian on the succession of George I. After the Hanoverian succession in 1714, the British government was a bear pit of factionalism and infighting and, in Scotland, power rested fairly consistently with the adherents and supporters of the Duke of Argyll.

Here lay some of the seeds of the Jacobite rising of 1745. There were some Whig clan chiefs loyal to the government who were not, however, part of the Argyll faction and they became more marginalised as time passed. Some of these, such as Grant of Grant, became neutral, while others, such as Cluny MacPherson, began the '45 in sympathy with the government but were swayed by the Prince's personal magnetism.

Lord Lovat had been a supporter of the Hanoverian succession since the beginning, albeit for personal advancement and financial and territorial gain. Now, however, consigned to the political wilderness and seeing what seemed to be the miraculous victories achieved by the Jacobite army, he mobilised the clan for Prince Charles that December. His son marched them to join the Prince at Stirling (allowing Lovat to be able to declare non-involvement) and they later took part in the Battle of Falkirk.

At Culloden, the Frasers fielded one of the largest regiments, led by Charles Fraser (Younger, of Inverallochie). They stood near the centre of the front line, charging with the other clan regiments and suffering similarly heavy losses.

After the battle, Charles Fraser, the regiment commander, was lying on the moor, badly wounded. One of the Hanoverian generals ordered a young aide-de-camp to shoot this fallen Jacobite. The captain refused, on a point of honour, and so a trooper was ordered to carry out this killing instead. General Hawley ('Hangman Hawley') is the most likely candidate to have given the order; he had a score to settle, having been defeated at Falkirk. The aide-de-camp involved was on Hawley's staff, a James Wolfe, later to become the famous General Wolfe.

Twelve years later, a regiment of 1,500 Frasers serving in the British Army was sent to Canada. They followed Wolfe loyally, due to his mercy to their leader on Culloden Field. It is said that when Wolfe fell wounded at Quebec, he died in the arms of a Fraser Highlander. The regiment was ultimately demobilised over there, leading to a large number of Canadian Fraser descendants. Many of them see a direct tie between Wolfe's refusal to shoot Charles Fraser and their own ancestors settling in Canada.

Old Simon Fraser, Lord Lovat, spent weeks after the battle hiding in a variety of refuges. He was finally captured on an island in Loch Morar and taken to the Tower of London. There, he achieved lasting notoriety as the last man to be beheaded by the axeman on Tower Hill and the last Peer of the Realm to be executed in

Britain. This 80-year-old schemer seems eventually to have made a choice, his final words being, '*Dulce et decorum est pro patria mori*'; it is sweet and fitting to die for one's country.

Many Frasers visit Culloden, to see where their ancestors fought and where some of them lie. Strangely, however, they are not the only visitors who ask for directions to the Fraser Stone. In 1991, an American writer, Diana Gabaldon, wrote a work of romantic fiction set in the Jacobite era, the hero of which is a clansman named Jamie Fraser. A sequel describes the Battle of Culloden and this has generated a significant number of literary visitors, who also come looking for the Fraser Stone. They view the stone with a certain respect, and so this interest is welcomed by genuine Frasers, who are happy to see the story of Culloden gain a wider audience in the world.

*The Clan Fraser Stone*

## The Grants of Glenmoriston and Glenurquhart

Clan Grant did not rise for Prince Charles. Whether it was raised for King George or not is a debatable point. The clan chief, Ludovick Grant, lived in Castle Grant, in Strathspey. Although he was Presbyterian, and Whig, his political enthusiasm was blunted, as he was out of favour with the powerful Argyll faction in the government.

He did send one independent company to Lord Loudon in Inverness, but, despite repeated requests, he kept the rest of his clansmen close to home, as protection from Jacobite raids. He did not have such tight control over the Grants in Glenmoriston and Glenurquhart, however, who rose in August 1745, joining Glengarry's Regiment in the Jacobite army. There were over a hundred men – mainly Grants, but including others – and they fought in all of the major engagements of the campaign.

About 30 of their number fell at Culloden, before they retreated from the field to a fugitive existence back in the glens. The survivors sought the advice of Ludovick, their chief. On his advice (and his promise of a safe return to their homes), they came into Inverness on 4 May to surrender themselves and their weapons to Cumberland.

His promise was broken, honour being a casualty in these times. These 16 men of Glenmoriston and 68 of Glenurquhart were marched down to Citadel Quay and loaded aboard the prison transport *Dolphin*. When they reached Tilbury, some were transferred to prison ship HMS *Pamela*.

Witnesses relate that over 400 men died in these prison hulks on the Thames. Such Grant prisoners as survived were eventually tried, then transported to Barbados. By 1750, only 18 of the original 84 were still alive.

Cumberland and Ludovick Grant each blamed the other for this violation of the safe-passage agreement for the rest of their lives.

Meanwhile, about seven of these eighteen men slowly but surely made their painstaking way home. Donald Grant was one of the lucky few and, on his return, he made sure he testified as to the fate of the others.

# The End of the Road to Drummossie Moor

We have heard now, in so many different accounts, that when the battle started government artillery pounded the Jacobites at long range until the front line began their last fateful charge. This reached the government lines at the southern edge of the conflict but was broken after savage hand-to-hand fighting. Elsewhere, the feared Highland charge did not even reach the government lines. Those clansmen ran into a hail of artillery fire and volleys from Brown Bess muskets long before they came close enough to use their dirks and broadswords.

The battle was over in under an hour – with perhaps 200–300 government troops killed or wounded, and an estimated 1,500 Jacobites dead. Many more were killed as they lay wounded on the battlefield. Government dragoons were dispatched to hunt down escaping Jacobites, and they cast a wide net, indiscriminately killing anyone who crossed their path. It is said that they created 'a broad river of the dead, all the way to Inverness'.

About 3,500 Jacobites were taken prisoner throughout the 45 Rising. Of these, 200 were executed or died in prison, while around 1,000 were transported to the colonies. Over 200 more were 'banished'. Many others were finally discharged, though the eventual fate of almost 700 of them will never be known.

Culloden, then, was the last engagement in the last attempt by the Jacobites to reinstate the Stuart dynasty through armed might. The Jacobite era, which had lasted almost 60 years, was over. However, the times of terror were just beginning.

The Duke of Cumberland was tasked with the job of 'pacifying' the Highlands, and so his occupying forces marched from garrisons at Fort William, Fort Augustus and the Isle of Skye. The time of burning, murder, rapine and pillage began. Even clans which had been loyal to George II fell prey to these redcoat patrols active in every glen. Houses were burned and livestock driven off and sold by the thousand. There is adequate evidence contained within sources such as letters, documents and journals with which to paint a picture of nearly a year of extreme brutality and suppression.

These military actions were bolstered by the actions of the State. Prohibitions and proscriptions were introduced concerning the bearing of arms, the wearing of tartan or kilts, the speaking of Gaelic and the playing of the pipes. Lands were forfeited and oaths of loyalty extracted:

> I do swear, as I shall answer to God at the great
> day of Judgement, I have not, nor shall have in my
> possession any gun, sword, pistol or arm whatsoever, and
> never use tartan, plaid, or any part of the Highland Garb;
> and if I do so may I be cursed in my undertakings,
> family and property,
> may I be killed in battle as a coward, and lie without
> burial in a strange land, far from the graves of my
> forefathers and kindred;
> may all this come across me if I break my oath.

This, then, was the way, and these were the measures used, to bring about the end of a way of life and a meaningful clan system. Now, 260 years later, the Highlands are quiet, and the National Trust for Scotland is guardian of the site at Culloden Battlefield and interpreter of the story.

The two single biggest misconceptions about the site that visitors sometimes have are: the battle was between the Scots and the English, and the battle was between Catholics and Protestants. Neither of these views is correct.

The 1745 Jacobite rising was a civil war – there were significant numbers of English on both sides, and large numbers of Scots, even Highlanders. There were Catholics and Protestants on both sides and, if a religious difference *was* apparent at all on this field, it was that Protestant Presbyterians tended to predominate among the government forces, while Protestant Episcopalians generally sided with the Jacobites.

The real division in this civil war was dynastic. The question being settled was whether Britain's throne was to be held by the House of Stuart or the House of Hanover. And although the House of Hanover was victorious, the most fascinating questions, as always in history, are the great what-ifs.

In this case, we might justifiably say that had the Jacobites won the '45 rising, the following seven decades of strife between Britain and France would have been avoided. Neither George III nor his madness would have ascended the throne, and without George's arrogance, or the necessity for high taxes from the colonies to pay for the French wars, the American Revolutionary War would never have happened. And what about the French Revolution? It too might have been avoided without the ongoing war with Britain creating a continual strain on the French economy and army.

And so, for these reasons and others, Culloden is significant.

As well as being the last battle on British soil, Culloden effectively marked the end of the clan culture in the Highlands. The proscriptions and the enlistments that followed – as soldiers were allowed to bear arms, wear tartan and play the pipes – set the scene for the enduring myth of the Scottish soldier; it can also be said that the changes in society ushered in the Highland Clearances.

Today, due to these powerful sets of factors, Culloden is viewed as an icon and a place of heritage pilgrimage to much of North America, Australasia and across Europe (the three continents referred to on page 59).

For me, that also makes it a story magnet. Every time the front door of the visitor centre creaks, it is another potential story walking in. If I use my ears and mouth in the proportions appropriate to their number, then I can gather amazing stories to fill the remaining pages of this book. Together they should create a fitting journal charting the shape of Culloden as battlefield, graveyard and heritage icon.

# PART THREE

# TALES BY WAY OF THE DOOR

## A Song of Proverbs

In ancient days, tradition says,
When knowledge much was stinted –
When few could teach and fewer preach,
And books were not yet printed –
What wise men thought, by prudence taught,
They pithily expounded;
And proverbs sage from age to age,
In every mouth abounded.

*O blessings on the men of yore*
*Who wisdom thus augmented,*
*And left a store of useful lore*
*For human use invented.*

– Charles, Lord Neaves

# Register of Tales

## A Story of Beginnings, and of Ships and Keys

It was February 2006. I had opened up the exhibitions area as usual and served the first few customers of the day. Being winter, it was quiet. It did not feel like a particularly portentous day. I was getting no vibes to the effect that something very special was about to happen.

The family grouping approaching me was no different to the standard visitors we normally welcome. There was a young lad of school age, his mum and his granny. They were particularly interested in knowing everything there was to know about MacGregors and their actions on the battlefield.

I did my usual research and showed them the appropriate pages in *No Quarter Given,* the Muster Roll of Prince Charles's army. I also cross-referenced *Culloden* by John Prebble and *Prisoners of the '45.*

Talk then turned to the name MacGregor in general, and their ancestors in particular. The senior member of the group explained how their family had emigrated to Canada in 1786 but had actually returned to Scotland to live a century or so later. She said that her great-great-great-grandfather, James MacGregor, had been the first Presbyterian Minister to serve Pictou, Nova Scotia. I then referred to the book *Scotland Farewell*, by Donald MacKay, which tells much of the history of Pictou. She was delighted when we managed to find the Reverend in question – so delighted, in fact, that she purchased the book!

James MacGregor was born in the Loch Earn area of Perthshire and later attended Edinburgh University and Alloa Theological School. It was the General Associate Synod of Scotland who, in 1786, chose him to go and preach on the Pictou River. Pictou was a community first settled 13 years earlier by the party travelling on that most famous of Highland emigrant ships, the *Hector*.

I paid very close attention as Mrs MacGregor began speaking of the *Hector*. That ship had long been an interest of mine. In fact, ever since a conversation with a previous visitor to Culloden in the early spring of 2002. At that time, a couple of Canadians had come a-visiting. One was a Mackay, the other named Todd Fraser. Todd showed me documentation which substantiated his descent from a relative of Simon Fraser of Lovat and, after some time chatting and sounding out my level of interest, he also chose to gift to me a number of photographs of the reconstructed emigrant ship the *Hector* located on Pictou River, Nova Scotia, and a facsimile of the original ship's manifest. This listing showed his ancestor among the emigrants – and there are certainly a number of Frasers, including one Simon Fraser.

This gift sparked my interest and in the intervening years I have always been interested to learn a little more about the *Hector* when I can. The single issue that makes her famous is that she is popularly regarded as the first-ever emigrant ship to carry a full load of passengers from the Highlands of Scotland to Nova Scotia. I found out more recently that one of the two partners behind the voyage of the *Hector* was John Witherspoon, one of the prime architects of the Declaration of American Independence – a well-loved preacher from Paisley, who had emigrated just five years earlier, in 1768.

Land and passage to America was offered at £3 5s per adult. The emigrants, from Wester Ross and Sutherland, were mostly from lands administered by the Board of Forfeited Estates following the 1745 Jacobite rising. These emigrants tended to be tenants, choosing to leave high rents and poor harvests behind. Around 200 of them sailed from Loch Broom in July 1773. It was a hard voyage: 18 of the children aboard would die of smallpox and dysentery before they made landfall in mid-September.

This was the background to my continuing conversation with Mrs MacGregor. She told me that although she was directly descended from the Reverend James MacGregor, it was from his second marriage. The Reverend James's first wife had actually been a passenger on the *Hector* – as a mere babe in arms called Ann Mackay. I wondered about the motivations behind Ann's family choosing to take ship for Pictou Harbour. As I knew that the enforced clearances in the Highlands did not begin wholesale until the 1790s, I asked her if it was an economic migration.

'Oh, no!' she replied. 'It's a far better story than that.'

And this is the story she told.

'Ann Mackay's father, Roderick, a fiery-tempered blacksmith from Beauly, was languishing in the Tolbooth Jail in Inverness in the year of 1773. He was a man who believed in the rights of the common man to distil his own whisky as he wished. So when he chanced across some government excise officers in the midst of a whisky seizure, he had tried to intervene. Bold though this may have been, it wasn't entirely wise, and this was the reason for his incarceration in Inverness Jail.

'As the days passed, Roderick struck upon a novel escape plan. He became friendly with the jailer and eventually persuaded that hapless individual to go and buy some strong drink – from Roderick's purse – so that they could have a drink to seal their friendship! It wasn't long before the jailer was sufficiently inebriated as to allow Roderick to help himself to the jail key and escape – conveniently locking the jailer in his own jail in the process.

'Looping by Beauly on his way west, Roderick picked up his wife, Christina, and his children, John and the infant Ann. Then they went hell for leather over the spine of the country to Loch Broom on the west coast. There, without delay, they boarded the *Hector* and left Ullapool – and the long arm of the law – behind. After a stormy passage, they disembarked at Pictou Harbour, Nova Scotia.

'Ann married James MacGregor twenty-three years later, in 1796, in Halifax and bore him seven children before her death in 1810. James then married for a second time, and it was some descendants from this second wife who chose to return to Scotland towards the close of the nineteenth century.'

Her story done, Mrs MacGregor stopped and looked to me for a reaction.

'That is a fabulous story!' I said. 'I hope you don't mind me asking, but is there any corroboration for that story?'

'Oh, yes,' she replied. 'When Roderick made his escape from the Tolbooth, he had the foresight to take the key with him; in fact, he took it all the way to Pictou Harbour and it rests to this day in the Public Archives of Nova Scotia in Halifax.'

Although it had not seemed like a very special day as I had opened up that morning, it had ended on a very different note and was the inspiration for this collection of Culloden tales.

## All Tied Up and No Place to Go

Many are the stories I have heard over the years at Culloden. Some of them are quite complex and detailed; others involve detective work, which is so satisfying when a real answer is turned up. Many are just snippets and, no matter how hard I look, I am unsuccessful in finding out any more for the person involved. I include one such scrap here and, if any reader can shed further light on this fragment, then please contact me through Mainstream, my publisher, and I will pass on the information.

The Whittakers, an elderly couple from Wellington, New Zealand, visited Culloden just before Easter 2006. There is a tradition that an ancestor of theirs was a Jacobite, a man called Peter Wilson from Ordiquhill, Banffshire. He was apparently captured by Cumberland in early April 1746, as the government army marched towards the Spey. Peter was tied to one of Cumberland's gun carriages by night and was forced to walk, bound, throughout the day. His eventual fate is unknown and, in this case, perhaps we have to accept that it is likely to remain so.

# No Compensation

It is easy to lose sight of the fact that the major military manoeuvrings at the time of Culloden did not just affect those who were taking part in the struggle but huge numbers of ordinary folk around and about. This was brought home to me in the autumn of 2005 when some National Trust for Scotland members, the Andersons, from near Alves, in Moray, came to the visitor centre. I began by explaining to them that the single biggest concentration of Andersons on the field was in Ogilvy's Regiment in the Jacobite second line. I then listened with interest as they told me of a letter which they had held in their family for centuries. It was from the British Army, dated 1746, informing their ancestors that there would be no compensation for the fields of crops trampled by Cumberland's troops. This was on the march westwards towards Culloden from their camp at Alves, where they had spent the night of 13 April.

The Andersons were also interested in what Bonnie Prince Charlie's approach to the 'small' folk was and so I looked up a very special source book. *The Lyon in Mourning* is a quite remarkable set of three volumes. It was compiled between 1746 and 1755 by Robert Forbes, later Bishop of Ross and Caithness. It comprises a collection of papers, correspondence, extracts from journals, etc. relating to the 1745 rising.

Within its detailed pages we found the household accounts, written by James Gibb, an excise officer from Leven who served Prince Charles as Master of Household. These accounts are a faithful recording of all the monies that Prince Charles paid on a day-to-day basis from his private income for provisioning. By comparing dates, we worked out that on the same day as Cumberland was requisitioning food without recompense, and his troops were trampling the Anderson crops, Bonnie Prince Charlie was in Inverness, paying cash for that day's goods and services:

| | |
|---|---:|
| To 13 load of pitts | 8s 3d |
| To poltrie and eggs | 7s 6d |
| To greens, roott, etc. | 2s 3d |
| To 1,800 oysters | 7s 6d |
| To Lady Kilrars servant and Mrs Donin's do | 2s 0d |
| To a hair | 0s 9d |
| To portage of river watter | 5s 7d |
| To a further 18 load of pitts | 12s 0d |
| To whit and oat bread | £1 17s 0d |
| To candles | £1 0s 0d |

Both sides of this tale shine a light on the continuing activities of the ordinary people, even in war, and each line of the above accounts represents the daily toil of some individual or family.

## The Night March

It was late June 2006. I was standing with my colleague, Duncan Cook, at the ticket desk when we were approached, a little hesitantly, by two ladies. I put their hesitation down to the fact that Duncan, being the 'living history' professional in the building, was dressed as an eighteenth-century soldier of France.

Undaunted, however, the ladies went on to ask their question: 'Could either of you tell us the route of Bonnie Prince Charlie's night march to Nairn the night before Culloden?'

The simple answer was 'Yes', within the limitations of historical sources. Duncan went to the shop to find a map of appropriate scale, while I gave a quick summary of the reasons for the night march and indeed its failure.

The Jacobites had known for almost a week that Cumberland was on his way from Aberdeen to force what he hoped would be a final, and successful, confrontation. There was no consensus among the Jacobite leadership on the best location for this impending clash. There was a feeling, however, that Drummossie Moor was not the finest choice. As the days slipped by, the number of options narrowed and, by 15 April, a plan was conceived whereby the

Jacobite army would attempt to march through the night and surprise the government army in the early hours of the 16th. (The 15th had been Cumberland's birthday and the hope was that, having enjoyed a break-out of the rum rations, the government forces might be less alert and more of a sitting target.)

The Jacobites began their march, in two divisions, at about 8 p.m., and they followed the route of the modern B9006 fairly closely, until driving rain, deepest darkness and the confusion of woodlands and walls confounded them a little to the north of Kilravock Castle. Here, things got strung out and confused, and Lord George Murray, commanding the first division, decided, at around 2 a.m., that the plan was flawed and unworkable. He peeled off to the north, passing through Croy, and returned to Culloden via Tornagrain. He seems to have perhaps achieved this without clearly letting the second division know what was happening. This second division, commanded by the Duke of Perth, continued their march towards Nairn, passing slightly north of Clephanton, until at around 2.45 a.m. they reached the Meikle Kildrummie area, where they could hear government sentries talking. At this point, they received word that the first division had turned back and were left with little option but to do the same. By 3 a.m., therefore, the woods were full of Jacobites, streaming back westwards in the direction of Culloden.

I paused for breath, my summary done, and with excellent timing Duncan returned with the map. This allowed us to plot for them the exact route that the night march had followed.

Suddenly, all animation, they were indicating a house near Clephanton on the map. 'That's my house! Right there!'

'Ah, well,' said Duncan, 'whoever was living there in 1746 would have been sure to have heard the night march going by.'

'Yes,' said one of the ladies, 'and we still do! Not often, mind you. Just about five times in the last ten years. It's the same every time. Woken in the early hours of the morning by the sound of large numbers of armed men going by. A few minutes of silence and then the noise of a tail-end charlie running hard to catch up, crossing the garden diagonally. Looking out, there's never a thing to be seen. Just the night air, echoing with the noise of an army from before, and a slightly frizzy feeling of electricity on the nerve endings.'

'Well, at least now you know it was the Duke of Perth's, heading for Nairn,' said Duncan.

Neither lady looked particularly as if that answered every question that might arise when coping with a ghost army. But they did thank us very kindly, nonetheless.

# The Clach an Airm

It was in late 2004 that a local man, a Mr Paul, came into the centre with his young daughter. He had not been in for some years and felt it was time he took his child so that she could learn a bit about her heritage.

Their family had long inhabited part of Strathnairn. Some of their ancestors had probably fought and fallen with Clan Chattan on 16 April, but obviously this man's particular line had seemed lucky enough to survive the time of fire and sword, and the Pauls therefore still enjoy being Starthnairn residents to this day.

We chatted for quite a while and then the topic of the Clach an Airm came up. I had never heard of this, so I pressed him for more information. His grandfather had told him the story of the Clach an Airm, the Stone of Swords. It was here, before the Battle of Culloden, that they sharpened their weaponry together, a communal activity designed to ready themselves psychologically for the coming conflict.

Mr Paul showed me the location of the stone on the map and then finished by telling me that if I wanted to know more then I should look up the Strathnairn Heritage Association website. I did just as he suggested and was pleased to find all the information I could want on the Clach an Airm.

It is not my habit within the pages of this book to use material verbatim from elsewhere, but in some instances I think it is justified. In this case, Drummossie is in Strathnairn, the men of Strathnairn are the local men who fell on the field, and the story on Strathnairn's website is the most fitting that I could hope to put on these pages as a tribute. So I sought permission from the heritage group, and from William Forbes, the author of the piece, in order to include most of it, as follows:

> Picture the scene. It is early morning on Tuesday, 15 April 1746. We are looking at a prehistoric standing stone located on a wide open landscape at Gask in the heart of Strathnairn. Apart from a few sprawling, mature Caledonian Scots Pine trees scattered at random across the countryside, there is very little shelter from the north-easterly breeze. The sky is dark and heavy and there is a feeling of winter in the air, even although it is springtime.
>
> All around is a babble of sound. There are people here – a lot of people. All are speaking in the Gaelic language of their ancestors. There is a feeling of anticipation that something very important is soon to take place. Alongside the voices there is a continuous sound of metal scraping on stone. Men are lining up to take turns to sharpen swords, dirks and spikes on their highly decorated targes [shields]. This prehistoric stone is the focal point of attention. These men are preparing to do battle with an, as yet, distant enemy. It is important that they are prepared. Their lives may depend on how well they have sharpened their weapons. Clach an Airm has been used for centuries to sharpen swords, knives, domestic utensils and agricultural implements. Today is probably the most important day in its existence.

Clach an Airm is a colourful scene this morning. There are hundreds of men gathering together, dressed in the tartan garb of their forebears. The colours are those of various dyes derived from vegetation growing wild in their neighbourhood. A few of the people present are obviously men of some standing in the community. It is easy to tell – they are the ones wearing fine jackets, continental shirts with lace trim, and expensive, decorative footwear. They are dressed for an occasion and many will look up to them for leadership as they face the enemy tomorrow some seven miles to the north-east. Amongst them are Captain Angus Mackintosh of Farr, Captain Farquhar MacGillivray of Dalcrombie and – the man who will lead the entire Clan Chattan regiment into battle – Colonel Alexander MacGillivray of Dunmaglass. The officers of this clan regiment are important men from important families in Strathnairn and surrounding areas. Their whole demeanour effuses authority – and today their authority will count for more than ever before.

The great majority of people here are not so well dressed, however. They are clothed in a simple but uniform attire – the long woollen plaid, a coarse homespun shirt and the distinctively Highland bonnet. The lucky ones have shoes – many are simply barefoot. Irrespective of whether these clansmen are rich or poor they share a common bond – one of kinship. They know their genealogies inside out. Some are here out of a determination to see Prince Charles Edward Stuart claim the throne of Great Britain once again for the Stuart dynasty – most people are here because they have to be. They would rather be tending their sheep, cattle and families. Refusal to turn up for the battle would result in their thatched roof being burnt and their cattle being confiscated by their landowning superiors.

So who are these men of the Clan Chattan gathered around this ancient landmark? Well, they are predominantly men from Strathnairn and Dores, although there are some from further afield. Most of them bear the surnames of families belonging to this ancient confederation of clans. There are Mackintoshes, MacBeans, Shaws, MacGillivrays and MacPhails. There are also other less common local names – Smith (or Gow), MacPherson, Forbes, etc. Many of these men have already walked a number of miles this morning and are glad of the rest and opportunity to talk to friends and relatives whom they have not seen for some time. Others – like John Mor MacGillivray, who farms here at Gask – have walked only a few hundred yards from their homes in this well-populated part of Strathnairn. Just on my left, now sharpening their swords, are 43-year-old Donald Forbes, who farms at Farr, Duncan Mackintosh from Aberarder and John MacPherson from Brin. They talk about the condition of their cattle and their plans for this year's crop cultivation while they scrape metal against stone.

The people gathered here are not men of any regulation 'military age'. Some are well on in years, having seen action as young men in the 1715 Jacobite Rebellion. Their knowledge and experience will be invaluable over the next two days. Others are young – very young – mere boys even, barely in their teens. Highlanders are natural soldiers, highly effective in warfare, armed for both distant and close combat, exceptionally mobile and – on their own territory – almost invincible. They will fight not only for their leader but – most of all – for their brothers, fathers, sons, cousins and uncles who stand alongside them in the affray. They will fight furiously and passionately. Not just for their own pride but for the protection and honour of their kin. The might of the British Army fears the Highland warrior more than any other they have ever done battle with.

There is a restlessness now amongst the gathering. Men form roughly into groups behind their leaders and head towards an area of open ground somewhere to the south and east of Inverness. They will reinforce a Jacobite army that has endured seven long months of warfare across mainland Britain, fighting and winning two major battles during that time.

The Highland soldiers waiting at Culloden Moor are cold, tired and hungry and are in no fit state to fight. The long, hard winter has taken its toll on them. Our men here are fresh, well fed and rested. They are well prepared for military action. The finest infantry in the British Army will greet the men of Clan Chattan with great fear and trepidation.

It is now almost 4 p.m. the following day. I see a scattering of men across Drummossie Moor. Some alone, others in small groups. All are in haste, gasping for breath, torn, tattered, blood-stained, blackened with gunpowder. Their eyes show trauma and deep anxiety. I speak to one man who continues on his way as he replies in a haphazard manner. I can barely make out his reply, but my worst fears are confirmed. The great anticipation and optimism of yesterday has now been replaced by a sense of hopelessness, fear and panic. The enemy has been victorious.

The men of Clan Chattan acquitted themselves well. But from what I can gather, the casualty rate has been enormous, many have been taken prisoner and those who have escaped now fear greatly the consequences of this defeat for themselves and their families.

I learn that, like so many others from this Strath, John Mor MacGillivray from Gask will never return home again to his native soil. Captain Angus Mackintosh was wounded on the battlefield – his fate is unknown. Donald Forbes was captured and is now imprisoned in a miserable Hanoverian prison ship awaiting transportation to the West Indies and to a life of slavery. Our courageous leader, Colonel Alexander MacGillivray, died bravely in the thick of the action as he urged his men forward against intense artillery and musket fire. Captain Farquhar MacGillivray, Duncan Mackintosh and John MacPherson have been much more fortunate – they all managed to escape to safety from the battle. Freedom, however, will be short-lived for Duncan and John – the redcoats will eventually hunt down and capture them on 7th of June. Safety for all others means a secure hideout in the hills with their families or – if you are one of the very few who has money – passage to France. There will be many anxious, hungry days, weeks and months ahead for those who lie low in the heather, awaiting the enemy search parties.

Some days have gone by. It is now late afternoon on Wednesday, 23 April 1746. All around are roofless cottages with smoke still rising from the burnt embers. Hanoverian soldiers still scour the landscape, killing defenceless people of all ages and gender, destroying property and gathering what remains of the livestock from the crofts and farms around the Clach an Airm. I cannot bear to recount the atrocities that I have seen carried out by these brutal and vengeful soldiers from the victorious army. They are out of control and bring shame on the name of the king they serve.

The Clach an Airm will remain standing where it has stood for many centuries. It will be seen for many generations yet to come. But the details of what I have witnessed happening all around the vicinity of this stone, during the days and weeks following the Battle of Culloden, will be lost from historical record for all time. The personal memories of these tragic events will die with the people who lived through them. The pain arising from what took place on 16 April 1746 at Culloden Battlefield, and its aftermath, however, will remain with Strathnairn forever.

# Bright Light, Strange Sight

'I had very little knowledge of my heritage until a couple of years ago. It was something that was not discussed around our house. I knew that my father's people came to America from somewhere in Angus, and my mother's people from Kintyre, and that's about it!'

So spoke the laconic elderly Westerner. It was the spring of 2006 when he arrived at the front desk. The horse that had rolled on him some years earlier had left him busted up in a variety of different ways. He walked with an obviously painful rolling hitch; his wife explained he was still in recovery. He wanted to know how far it was around the whole field – they both impressed upon me the importance they attached to being able to see it all. He was fiercely independent but, after a little persuasion, agreed that our mobility scooter would help him to see what he wanted – and might even be fun at the same time.

An hour or so later, I met them at the door, as they returned from the field. They really appreciated the extra range that the vehicle had given them. Their delight at seeing the whole field may have been what led them to tell a story previously only shared within their family. Or maybe it was just the right time and the right place for a little bit of disclosure.

The story was both powerful and strange. It demanded attention due to its compelling blend of medical drama, life-and-death struggle and inexplicable phenomena. And its strength lies in the ultimate scepticism of its teller.

As he got off the scooter, he seemed just a bit baffled. He said that he didn't understand why there were trees everywhere, nor did he understand the lack of any view of the sea. The place should be flatter, and perhaps wetter.

I explained that what he had been describing was a very accurate representation of the field as it would have looked on the day of the battle. Many eyewitnesses wrote that 'there were no trees as far as the eye could see', which in turn meant that the sea was visible, together with the navy ships, watching the battle through telescopes. The mid-eighteenth century was a wetter period and so ground water would have been greater. And finally, the area was grazed pasture, and so any heather or meadow grass would be much shorter than that seen these days. But without advanced in-depth study and understanding of the battle, I could not see how he would know these things. Here is what he told me:

'I was raised around horses, but after college just never had time for them – too busy with business and family. So it wasn't until later in life that we decided to get some horses, including one nice-looking Arab gelding with a vicious streak. I didn't think he could buck me off, which it transpired was a major misjudgement on my part. I suspected he might have been mistreated, as I had to start his training from scratch.

'He was starting to come round but was still a little highly strung. It was one summer's day in the late '90s that my wife and I were going for a ride. My wife's horse ducked out of the gate and headed south. Without thinking, I tossed a rope onto the saddle of my Arabian and stuck my foot in the stirrup. Before I could get my leg over him, he took off at a run. We were in the process of building a new house and the leach field was full of loose dirt. It had rained a couple of days before and the ground was muddy. When he hit the mud, it scared him and he started bucking. In the process, he lost his footing. I could feel him going down and tried to push off and get away from him. I really thought I had made it. I remember hitting the ground and must have blacked out for just a few seconds.

'When my wife got there, I told her we would go to town for an X-ray. By the time we got to the highway, I knew I was in trouble. I lost consciousness before we got to town and have no recollection of the next four days. They examined me at the local hospital, finding the ribs on my right side broken, my lung and diaphragm punctured, and my liver and spleen cut up. I spent the next six weeks in intensive care and during that time have very few recollections of things going on around me. I don't know how many times they told my wife I wasn't going to make it.

'When I finally got home, a neighbour told my wife that she had seen the accident, and that the horse had rolled over on me. I had no memory of that happening.

'Over the next year or so, I would start to get flashbacks of things that happened at the hospital. Probably the most significant time was when doctors told my wife not to bother calling anyone who was further than three hours away, as that was the maximum time I had. I saw a bright light as in a tunnel and remember going into the tunnel. I emerged at the other end and, when I came out, I was on a high piece of ground, looking to the west, and below was a large group of men separated into groups. They were in Highland kilts, but no particular colour. There were perhaps ten or more very faded battle flags and I could see water in the distance. This faded out and the same view was of a large flat area with some large, round, smooth rocks sticking out of the ground by a foot or two, and lots of bushes with white or pink flowers. The rocks were smooth and had moss on them. Scattered across the area were large mounds that didn't seem to match the existing terrain.

'Over the following weeks, I would have the same visions from time to time, depending upon pain in a particular area, though they finally quit after a year or two.

'My youngest son got into the Scottish heritage mode a few years ago and, although I had never told anyone other than my wife about these things up until then, I thought he might find it interesting. My son had a friend from Scotland, who said what I saw was Culloden. At that point, I had never heard of Culloden.

'As time passed, I did some reading on the area. The more I thought about it, the more I wanted to see it. As I can't sit upright for very long, or walk for a distance, I didn't think I could make the trip. It's amazing what can be done when you try. We finally got here. As to Culloden, it seems smaller. I suppose the trees make that difference, or perhaps the large mounds of earth not being present. I wish I could say that I felt something as I looked at the stones marking the clan graves. If I did, then it was just a little sadness at all that had subsequently flowed from this small bit of ground.'

Determination has been one of the central strengths pulling this man through his convalescence. He is also defined, however, by a gritty pragmatism and a belief in the power of human decency. These are the qualities I see rising to the surface when he summed things up thus: 'I don't know if this information is of any benefit. I haven't told anyone outside the family, except you, about these occurrences. They don't make a lot of sense to me, nor do I expect others to believe them or care whether they do or not. My father's people were shipped out due to the 1745 rising, and my mother's people probably left shortly after as a result of economic necessity. However, in the final analysis, it seems clear to me that it is not what happened to your forefathers that is most important but what you have done with your own life.'

## A Courageous Stand

There was one summer day in 2004 when three North American ladies approached the front desk. Two of them were quite self-assured. They wanted to know more about their clans. The first was a MacDonald, the second a Cameron. They knew a lot about their heritage and we were able to add a bit more, in terms of information about their clans' actions on the field. The third lady was a great deal more diffident than her friends. She came forward only reluctantly and asked, almost apologetically, about her clan name. It was MacBean and, unbelievably, she had been told by some ignorant acquaintances in the past that it was not really a clan at all! I was delighted to tell her that it was not only a proper clan but also an ancient one, with a heroic past.

I explained that the MacBeans were a local clan, from the northeast end of Loch Ness. In fact, as recently as 1961 the 21st chief, Hughston McBain of McBain, acquired a magnificent elevated site above Dores, with stunning views down Loch Ness and the Great Glen, and it was on this land that the McBain Memorial Park was, thereafter, created.

Then I pointed out the large painting on the wall opposite us. It was a representation of one of the Jacobite heroes at Culloden – Gillies MacBean. A man of around 6 ft 4 in., it is thought that as well as being the clan chief's son, he was also the innkeeper and tacksman at Dalmagarry, between Moy and Tomatin. He was a major in the Clan Chattan Regiment raised by Lady Mackintosh, and the painting shows him staunchly holding a breach in a wall against government forces. Lord Robert Kerr is also shown, lying mortally wounded.

These representations are, in actuality, more of a collage of incidents occurring at different points in the battle. The Clan Chattan Regiment charged the government's left flank, where an eyewitness account describes the fall of Captain Lord Robert Kerr of Barrell's Regiment, 'his head being cleft from crown to collarbone' by Major Gillies MacBean.

When the charge faltered, Gillies, who was already attacking the second line, was wounded by bayonet and laid low by a savage blow from a musket-stock. Rising weaponless, he realised that to save himself he would have to follow his retreating comrades.

He covered less than half a mile before being brought to bay by pursuing dragoons. There, near the farm steading of Balvraid, he armed himself with the 'tram', or haulage shaft, of a cart and placed his back to a wall. Facing his attackers, he fought with ferocity and defiance until the Cavalry Commander, the Earl of Ancrum, called out, 'Save the brave fellow!' The dragoons, however, enraged by his resistance, ignored this cry and rode him down.

In Peter Anderson's book, *Culloden Moor and the Story of the Battle*, published in 1867, he writes:

> Though left for dead, Gillies was found still in life and conscious by an old woman from one of the houses, who covered him, at his own desire, with straw; but he died shortly after . . . The house was one of several there at the time and stood within what is now the corn-yard. He was buried beside it and a large stone laid over him; but his friends later removed the body.

The warlike prowess shown at Culloden was not just the preserve of MacBeans from the eighteenth century. In 1858, a descendant, Major-General William MacBean, was to receive the Victoria Cross for the dispatch of 11 men in the main breach at Lucknow, India.

The American lady was also pleased to receive a copy of the Clan MacBean leaflet from us and so to read about the clan's tartan. It is the only tartan to have gone to the moon: in 1969, astronaut Alan Bean, the fourth man to walk on the moon, took a length of the tartan on Apollo 12's journey. Half of the material was left on the moon as a flag, while the remainder was returned for the clan archives!

Assimilating all of this information, our American guest said, 'Well, there's only one thing left to do, then. I'll have to purchase that picture of Gillies MacBean, the hero, holding the breach in the wall. It'll go on my chimney-breast when I get home and anytime anyone with less sense than roadkill tells my kids that they aren't part of a real clan, well, I'll just refer them to Gillies!'

# Covering the Retreat

At Culloden, many people ask whether we know if anyone of their name fought in the battle. If the answer is yes, then we are, understandably, often asked for further details. Some names are immediately known to us – for example, we have heard that the largest number of Andersons on the field served in Ogilvy's Regiment; the Reids, being a Sept of Robertson, are to be found principally in the Atholl Brigade; and MacKenzie is the most common name in the Earl of Cromartie's Regiment.

At other times, we are told names that we have never heard of in relation to the battle and a search through some of the old books begins. Sometimes we will be lucky and find examples, other times we regretfully have to inform our visitor that we cannot find any written evidence mentioning the surname in question. I felt the latter outcome would be the most likely when, back in 2001, a man approached the front desk with just such an enquiry.

'Hi, I'm ashamed to say that this is my first time visiting Culloden. I've often passed, but, you know, work . . . I was always in a rush. So I promised myself, the next time I'm passing, with even a wee bit of time to spare, I would pop in. I want to check out a story my grandpa told me before he died. He said our family fought for the Stuart cause in the 1745 rising. In fact, he said more. He told me that our regiment covered Bonnie Prince Charlie's retreat. I never paid much heed and it does seem unlikely, given that we don't even have a Highland name. My name is Potts, William Potts.'

I took out a copy of *No Quarter Given*, the Muster Roll. It was September, so we were still fairly busy, and I did not have time to search through the entire book for him. I explained that the names were not arranged alphabetically from beginning to end, instead being alphabetised within each rank and regiment. I said that I would open the book at random and give him just a little training on how to use it. He was content, after my example, that I would leave him to do his own research.

Then, recalling something important, he said suddenly, 'Ah, my grandfather also told me that our name spelling has changed over the years. It used to be spelt with an "E", instead of an "O".'

At that same moment, the book fell open, completely randomly, at page 92. As I was running my finger down the names, just to show him how to search for a 'P' name amongst other ranks, I suddenly saw it. Nestling between Francis Pecassan and Anthony Poo, there it was! And he saw it at the same time.

'But that's it!' he cried. 'William Petts! It's even the same first name as mine. So what regiment is that?' he wanted to know.

'The Royal Ecossais,' I told him, 'Lord John Drummond's French Regiment, comprising some French nationals but mostly recruited from Scots in exile at the court of Louis XV of France.'

'And what part did they play at Culloden?' was his next question.

'Well,' I said, 'your grandfather, it seems, was right in all aspects of his story. The French and Irish troops were among the regiments that stood firm at Culloden when the Highland charge faltered and broke.

'The Royal Ecossais engaged the Argyll Militia in a firefight around the walls of the Culwhiniac enclosure and, by standing firm and laying down musket volleys, they delayed the pursuing dragoons. They suffered heavy losses but were successful in covering Bonnie Prince Charlie's retreat.'

William Potts left a happy man, knowing now that his grandfather had passed him true family knowledge, which had somehow been preserved, and passed down, for almost 250 years.

# Flotsam and Jetsam

There are a number of different definitions for flotsam and jetsam. One that is particularly apt for our purpose is 'goods of potential value, floating on the open sea'.

It is amazing just how many items relating to the Jacobite risings still exist, and even more surprising is how many of them are still 'floating around' undocumented.

A New Zealander visiting Culloden once told me that the biggest collection of basket-hilted broadswords that he had ever seen was hanging on the wall of one of his work colleagues back home. We have, over time, been offered eighteenth-century paintings, Jacobite medals, letters and documents, and weaponry. Much of it is authentic, and there is often a story attached.

It was in June of 2005 that I was asked to give a presentation and battlefield tour for members of Clan Donald who were visiting Culloden. It was while we were down at the Clan Donald Stone that one of the company quietly, almost surreptitiously, took out a coin to show me. It was a louis d'or of a date that lent weight to the gentleman's story that it was part of Bonnie Prince Charlie's treasure. Said to be at least £38,000 in gold, this treasure was delivered by French ship to the shores of Loch nan Uamh, left there unclaimed and later reputedly buried somewhere in the general vicinity of Loch Arkaig. The gentleman in front of me, a Mr Allan from the USA, was now presenting the coin and asking me if I wanted to hold it. He said that a family tradition hints that prior to its burial small amounts of the treasure had made its way into the hands of some local families in the West Highlands. The coin I was now holding had been taken by his ancestor, as a precious keepsake, upon emigrating from Scotland. I thanked him for the tale and returned the coin, which he reverently placed back inside its case within his wallet.

Some of the letters we are shown at Culloden are simply domestic correspondence of the time, though they are also enlightening in the asides they make with reference to the military campaigns of both protagonists on the field.

The summer of 2005 brought the Whitmores to Culloden. They were pleased that they had come, and got more from their visit than expected. They asked some perceptive questions about the political background to Jacobitism in Britain and were also interested in who might have fought in Bonnie Prince Charlie's army.

Happy with information received, they told the story of a snuff mull they own. Some friends had inherited a London house and its contents in the '60s, they said. The prior owner had been an elderly lady by the name of Murray. One artefact in the house looked like an old powder horn and was the snuff mull. It was claimed it had been carried by the lady's ancestor at the Battle of Culloden. The Whitmores had particularly admired this object, and their friends gifted it to Mrs Whitmore some years later.

When questioned about how they knew this background to the horn, they produced an accompanying family tree, showing the lady to have been born in 1884, daughter of a J.A. Campbell Murray. The lineage then extends back into the eighteenth century. They also showed me an old parchment, which had been wrapped up securely inside the mull. It was written by Mr J.A. Campbell Murray and reads:

> This Snuff Mull belonged to my Grandmother, Grace Murray, and was carried by her father in the Battle of Culloden, 1745. Her maiden name was Stuart.

Although the date for the battle is wrong, it is an understandable error, still made by many people to this day. And there is nothing to suggest that the mull is not entirely genuine.

The Whitmores, impressed with the stewardship at the battlefield, have been good enough to offer to donate the snuff mull, feeling that Culloden is where it belongs.

# The Story of the Cairn

It was a visitor by the name of Farquharson who asked us, in 2003, whether our main memorial cairn at Culloden was inspired by the custom of the Highland Battle Cairn. He had come over from Australia in order to do some family research and to visit places of particular significance in his family background.

Just the day before, he had been to see that most poignant part of his Farquharson heritage, the Cairn na Cuimhne, which translates as 'the Cairn of Remembrance'. This cairn can be found on the north bank of the River Dee, just less than a mile upstream from Balmoral Castle.

He said that it had been a bit of an expedition, as nowadays a fence has to be clambered over in order to access the cairn. Any minor discomfort was worth the suffering, though, he reckoned, because of what the cairn represented and what it meant, to both him and his people.

The Farquharson Cairn is a particularly good example of an old, and emotive, Highland custom – that each clansman, upon being called to arms and prior to a battle, would bring with him a stone to the gathering place. This he would add to the growing pile laid by the others. When the battle was over, every surviving clansman who returned would carry away a stone from the roughly made cairn and the heap that remained was the indication of the number of men who had been killed.

The question that we had just been asked, therefore, was whether the Memorial Cairn at Culloden symbolised the same thing – the number of men lost. As it stands approximately 20 feet in height and about 18 feet in diameter at the base, it seems entirely possible, and appropriate, that this cairn *could* stand for all of those clansmen who never returned home, from either Culloden or the 1745 rising in general.

Almost before the last cannon fired, the battlefield was exerting a strong pull upon those people who wished to view this tragic site. With the exception of distraught family, the first visitors in those days of mid-April 1746 were scavengers or those with a ghoulish fascination for such scenes of violent death. Later visitors arrived with greater respect. Some of them sought to understand the background to the battle, while others came to visit the graves of the fallen – of both sides. This last aspect prompted thinking on whether there should be a cairn of remembrance, a memorial, on the field – and, if so, what form it should take.

The first plans took shape at the time of the centenary of the battle in 1846. The proposed Culloden Monument was designed by Alexander Mackenzie of Elgin and begun in 1849. It was described in the *Illustrated London News* as

> a gigantic cairn or artificial rock, the top of which will be accessible by flights of rustic steps and winding paths. Various spots will be so formed that tablets and small monuments to particular clans or individuals may at any time be erected.

Unfortunately, the money ran out before the structure reached 12 feet and the project was then shelved.

It was almost ten years later that a Jacobite named Edward Power donated a stone, inscribed 'Culloden 1746 – E P fecit 1858'. This was to be incorporated in another cairn being contemplated at that time.

That cairn never materialised, but Edward's stone was eventually embedded in the 1881 memorial erected by Duncan Forbes of Culloden. This is the monumental cairn that graces the site to this day. As a memorial, it has a sombre dignity, and it is likely to continue to be the focus for the annual anniversary service organised by the Gaelic Society of Inverness on the Saturday closest to 16 April. Attended by descendants of the fallen from all corners of the globe, this service enhances the memorial as a true cairn of remembrance.

# The Blind Fiddler

It was near the end of the day, in spring 2006. I was getting ready to lock up the building when I was engaged in conversation by a couple just as they were leaving. The best stories often present themselves when least expected and this was no exception.

The gentleman introduced himself as Robert (Robin) Robertson, a retired general medical practitioner. He proceeded to tell me of the adventures of his great-grandfather's great-grandfather, also a Robert Robertson. This young man had fought at Culloden, at the age of about 25, but survived to live a long and interesting life (including becoming known later as 'the Blind Fiddler of Dundee').

I asked if I could retell the story here, and Dr Robertson agreed, on two conditions. The first was that the tale be told simply, with no embellishments. The tale had first been researched and written up by his father's cousin, R.H.S. Robertson (1911–99) who, as well as having a glacier named after him, was successor to Sir Compton Mackenzie as president of the Scottish Patriots. He was a consulting mineralogist and author dedicated to improving industry in Scotland.

The second condition was to ensure that R.H.S. Robertson's surviving family, especially Mrs Robertson, were content with its inclusion. Happily she is comfortable with the idea of this tale reaching a wider audience and is delighted that it is to be included.

Robert Robertson was born in the parish of Moulin in 1721 and attended school there, probably learning English, Gaelic, arithmetic and some Latin. It is thought that his father was a tacksman on the Fergusson Estate of Balghulan.

Jacobitism would have had particular relevance to anyone born near Blair Atholl in the early eighteenth century but more so if you were a Robertson and your chief was Alexander Robertson of Struan, 'the Poet Chief', a man who had never acknowledged the

Houses of Orange or Hanover. This chief had attended St Andrews University (where he won the Silver Arrow by shooting arrows over St Rule's Tower) and the Sorbonne in Paris, and had been active during the main Jacobite risings. He was a veteran of '89 and the '15 and '45.

In 1689, houses in Moulin were burned by Royalist forces. This was in response to local support for Graham of Claverhouse – something that would not have been forgotten by Robert's parents. The Scots Parliament re-established Presbyterianism in 1690 and, in Robert's time, successive ministers in Moulin were Presbyterian. The Robertsons were Episcopalian (another marker of Jacobite tendency) and worshipped at the private chapel at Old Faskally House or at Kilmaveonaig.

In 1728, Walter Stewart became parson to this congregation. He was a strong Stuart supporter and was 'non-juring', which meant that he refused to swear the Oath of Allegiance to the King in London. It was a penal offence at the time for any clergyman to officiate where nine or more persons were present in addition to the household without praying for King George and abjuring the exiled Stuarts. Being an Episcopalian at that time had both a religious and a political side.

Robert's cousin, Charles Alexander, became the chief's factor, which probably brought Robert into closer contact with the chief, too. Little is known about Robert's life before 1745, except that he married his wife, Janet, in 1741 and had become a talented musician and a well-known fiddler by 1745.

The Royal Standard was raised at Glenfinnan on 19 August 1745 and, 12 days later, Prince Charles arrived at Blair Castle. He attended a dance at the House of Lude on 2 September, cheerfully dancing several reels and minuets. The first reel he called for was 'This is no mine ain house'. Robert may well have played that night.

A battalion of Athollmen joined the Prince in Edinburgh, arriving at camp on 19 September. The seventy-five-year-old Poet Chief, Alexander Robertson of Struan, led his hundred Robertsons to the Battle of Prestonpans two days later, and Robert was among them.

After the battle, Lord George Murray marched to Cockenzie and took possession of General Sir John Cope's baggage and stores. Cope's flight is remembered in the taunting song, 'Hey Johnnie Cope, are ye wauken yet?'

Prince Charles allocated shares of the captured equipment, and the Robertsons' portion included Cope's military coach and its contents. Struan was driven back to his home at Carie, near Rannoch, in the coach, wearing the general's fur-lined coat. Robert's share of the loot included a brace of fine pistols and, as he was known as a musician, he also received Cope's travelling fiddle, or 'kit'.

The coach and its contents had one more surprise in store for the clansmen. In one of the coach pockets, they found a brown substance which they thought was compressed snuff. I would not have liked to see their faces when they realised they were trying to snort chocolate, a substance they would have had no prior knowledge of.

The campaign in England and the retreat are well known. Six hundred Athollmen were also at the Battle of Falkirk on 17 January 1746.

During the retreat of 1746, Hanoverian troops occupied the country around Atholl. Lord George Murray, with many Clan Robertson men, surprised enemy garrisons throughout Atholl, sent round the Fiery Cross to raise more men and proceeded to besiege Blair Castle. He then marched northwards with the Athollmen, including Robert and his cousin, Charles, towards the Battle of Culloden, which changed all their lives forever.

The Atholl Brigade was on the right flank at Culloden under Lord George Murray.

John Alexander Robertson wrote, on 7 January 1904, from 34 Bonnygate, Cupar, to his son, Robert Robertson:

> My father in a conversation I had with him not long before he died said that it was handed down that his Great Grandfather, Robert Robertson, did great service at Culloden, where he watched at a slap of a dyke where a number of Cumberland's troopers were trying to get through and gave a good number of them their quietus.

Eventually, he was wounded. Murray managed to withdraw the remaining Athollmen in good order as far as Ruthven Barracks. John Alexander Robertson also wrote:

> Robert had many exciting escapes from Cumberland's soldiers, but by sleeping by day among the heather and travelling by night he finally got home to Moulin, where he made a hole in the thatch of his house and hid his sword, pistols and dirk where they remained until the country quieted down.

Apparently, his wounds were not too serious, but he was still in trouble. Being a Jacobite fugitive meant suffering the cold and damp of a Highland April, and being in constant danger of losing one's life to any of the frequent redcoat patrols.

Robert did not dally in Moulin but headed south to Birnam Wood, which was to be his hideout for at least nine months. Rohallion Estate, on Birnam Hill, had been a hiding place for emissaries from Rome after the Reformation. It is possible that he and Charles Alexander hid not too far from Alexander's home near Murthly and bundles of food were conveyed by trusted relatives and friends. Unfortunately, one lass who brought food also carried smallpox, which Robert contracted. He was blinded by it, a recognised complication of the disease, the biggest killer of eighteenth-century Europe. It is possible that he was given shelter afterwards by relatives, since he may no longer have been recognisable as someone who had been out during the '45.

On 9 February 1747, the Revd Adam Fergusson of Moulin wrote:

> There is now no Rebell of any consideration skulks in
> any part of Atholl that I know off. Strowan (the Chief)
> keeps to Rannoch still and drinks his whiskey as usual,
> except that he runs to the Hills or Wood, as do all the
> other guilty parties, when at any time any party of the
> Troops begin to stir in quest of them, which is not very
> often.

The following May, Commissar Bisset and Revd Adam Fergusson
carried in a great quantity of arms from the common people in the
country, who were forced out to the rebellion, but they did not
find Robert's weapons.

Unable to work or ply a trade in Moulin due to his blindness,
Robert kept up his music and enquiries were made about posts in
Lowland towns. When his chief, Alexander Robertson of Struan,
died in 1749, he may well have felt that his ties of loyalty to the clan
were lessened and that he was free to leave the Highlands and seek
a new life as a blind musician.

The clan system was ending. He now felt it safe enough to apply
to the minister of Moulin, the Revd Fergusson, for a testificate, a
certificate of respectability, to assist him on his way to Dundee, where
he had obtained a post as musician.

Adam Fergusson must have known that Robert had been an active
Jacobite and could have refused him a letter of recommendation.
However, while the minister did not approve of the rebellion, his
own position in Moulin must have been difficult and he may well
have tried to act in as humane and compassionate a way as possible
to all his flock. So, in May 1749, he issued the following testificate
to Robert:

> These are testifyeing to All concerned that the bearer
> hereof, Robert Robertson, a blind Laad, was born in
> this Parish of Mouline of honest parents; and resided
> in it from his Infancy till of late Years, behaving himself

honestly and soberly, free of all Church Censure and Scandal known to us. Wherefore he is recommended to the Reception and Kindness of any Christian Family or Congregation, where Providence may cast his lot.

> Given at Straloch, May 15th 1749.
> By appointment at the Session of Mouline.
> By Adam Fergusson, Minister of Mouline.

A testificate would have had no value if issued by a dissenting minister and Robert would have had to apply for one from his parish minister. (Few such certificates survive and a copy of this one is preserved in the Scottish Records Office.)

And so to Dundee with young wife Janet and their two children, Robert and William. His new employer was John Jenkins, 'Dancing Master' and 'Master of Manners'. He did return, later, to Moulin to collect his sword, dirk and Johnnie Cope pistols – a risky adventure. His sword was passed down the family and is now in the possession of Robert Robertson in Australia.

Janet died in 1756 and he then married Christian Drummond. They had a daughter in 1757. He named her Margaret Stuart Sobieski Robertson. Prince Charles Edward's mother was Princess Maria Clementina Sobieski. This illustrates where his sympathy still lay over ten years after the defeat at Culloden.

Margaret was musical, too, and played the classics in addition to the dance tunes required at work, where her father became known as 'the Blind Fiddler of Dundee'. In 1760, Jenkins loaned Robert £70 to buy the third floor of a tenement in the city. Jenkins bought the second floor, so they probably got on. Dancing, balls and assemblies had become very popular in the latter part of the century and there was a great demand for Robert's services.

Christian died in 1776 and so later that year he married his third wife, Agnes Coupar. They had a son called Charles. Gradually, Robert acquired more property and also became a merchant, assisted by his family, especially his son Robert.

Robert Robertson, musician, died on 9 May 1808, in Dundee, aged 87. His tombstone can be found in The Howff, Dundee's city cemetery. His third wife, Agnes, died in 1815.

Robert had a long and eventful life, involving both the Jacobite rising and the last battle to be fought in Britain. He was fortunate to survive both the battle and the worst atrocities ever carried out by the British Army. He was a strong man who, despite blindness, went on to become a successful father, musician and merchant.

And Johnnie Cope's travelling fiddle and pistols? As noted, Robert was given them after Prestonpans. The fiddle was narrow and could be slipped into a long frock-coat pocket. This kind of instrument was also known as a dancing master's fiddle. It was made in either Italy or Bohemia and authorities agree it dates from around 1720. It has been handed down the family since then.

In 1903, the fiddle was repaired and was exhibited in Edinburgh around the time of the First World War. It had a lucky escape in 1950 when left for repair at a Glasgow shop that was burgled and the safe blown, causing much damage. Fortunately, the fiddle was neither harmed nor stolen. It was taken to the BBC and Ian Whyte, the conductor, was excited by it. It was played on a Gaelic broadcast, but when the BBC asked if it could be played to a wider audience, R.H.S. Robertson replied, 'No, not until Scotland is free!'

We do not know what happened finally to the pistols. Robert's grandson – also Robert – was a staunch Tory. During the notorious days of the passing of the Reform Act in 1832, he fought the losing cause with such enthusiasm that ardent reformers gathered in front of his house in Cupar and, with long brooms, swept down his front walls to signify their desire to sweep all Tories from the town. Many people had their windows broken and apparently Robert's grandson kept the mob at bay by brandishing the pistols at them! What a contrast to today's docile voters.

And there ends the tale – told, I hope, with no frills and no embellishments. I am sure you will agree with me, and with the Robertsons, when we say it needs none. It is a tale that speaks for itself.

## Echoes from the Cathedral

Francis Townley joined the Jacobites at Preston on 27 November 1745. His ancestral home, Townley Hall, was in Lancashire, but he had left it, aged about 20 years, in 1728. He had taken up a military commission in the French Service, where he remained for many years. He returned to live in Wales not long before Prince Charles landed in Scotland. Three days after enlisting at Preston, Francis was given the rank of colonel and granted command of the newly raised Manchester Regiment.

Less than a month later, the Jacobites entered Carlisle on their retreat north from Derby. There were a number of dispatches awaiting Prince Charles, indicating growing support and more men back in Scotland. There was also news of more troops and artillery from France landing in the north. The fateful decision was therefore made to temporarily leave 400 men behind, to hold Carlisle as a gateway to England. It was not an easy decision, and certainly far from unanimous – the best that can be said for it is that it was taken in the mistaken belief that the Jacobite army would return to relieve these men in a few short weeks. Francis Townley requested most firmly that his Manchester Regiment be allowed to comprise part of the force chosen to defend the city.

The main force marched north for Scotland on 20 December. The garrison left behind did not have a few short weeks: Cumberland quickly requisitioned heavy artillery from Whitehaven and brought it to bear on the beleaguered town. In a matter of days, these 18-lb cannons battered and breached the walls and, on 30 December, the defenders finally decided to surrender forthwith.

Townley was imprisoned in the city gaol, but about 350 of the other ranks were imprisoned in the cathedral. They languished there for 12 days, many of them dying before the survivors were moved elsewhere.

It was in 2003 that a lady in her 80s by the name of Whitelees visited Culloden. She had been raised on tales of Jacobites told by her grandfather. He had worked at Carlisle Cathedral and the story of the Jacobite prisoners was familiar to him.

He had told her how it took more than a month of intensive cleaning, and burning of sulphur, and then aromatics, before the building was fit for services again. He also told her the names, and the ultimate fate, of some of the prisoners. Among these was, of course, Francis Townley. He was sentenced to death for treason and was the first of a party of nine Jacobites to be hung, beheaded and disembowelled on Kennington Common, London, on 30 July 1746.

The final story her grandfather had told her was not a story at all; it was a song. Entitled 'Townley's Ghost', it had been well known to those who worked in the cathedral at that time. Miss Whitelees was happy to offer a copy of the lines of this song from the notebook where she, herself, had written it prior to her grandfather's death:

### Townley's Ghost

When day in shades of night was lost,
And all was fast asleep,
In glided murdered Townley's ghost
And stood at William's feet.

Awake, infernal wretch, he cried
And view this mangled shade,
That in thy perjured faith relied
And basely was betrayed.

Embraced in bliss, and bathed in ease,
Tho' now thou seem'st to lie,

My injured form shall gall thy peace,
And make thee wish to die.

Fancy no more in pleasing dreams
Shall frisk before thy sight,
But horrid thoughts and dismal screams
Attend thee all the night.

Think on the hellish acts thou'st done,
The thousands thou'st betrayed,
Nero himself would blush to own
The slaughter thou hast made.

Not infants' cries nor parents' tears
Could stay thy bloody hand,
Nor could the ravished virgins' fears
Appease thy dire command.

But ah! What pangs are set apart
In hell, thou'lt quickly see,
Where even the damned themselves will start
To view a friend like thee.

In haste, affrighted, Willie rose
And trembling stood and pale,
Then to his cruel sire he goes
And tells the dreadful tale.

Cheer up, my dear, my darling son,
(The bold Usurper said)
Do not repent what thou hast done,
Nor be at all afraid.

If we on Scotland's throne can dwell
And reign securely here,
Your uncle, Satan, is king in hell
And he'll secure us there.

One final twist in this tale is that these echoes from 1746 can still be felt in England, too. Land forfeiture was one of the measures taken by the government in the aftermath of the Jacobite rising. It was not just the Scots estate owners who lost their lands; as might be expected, any of the English aristocracy who supported the House of Stuart also lost their lands. So when the Stuart cause failed, the Townley lands were forfeit, and his family were set to wandering, landless, on the byways of England . . . as some of their descendants still do. This explains why Townley is a not uncommon name among English travelling people today.

## Antigua and the Caribbean

Culloden, on a breezy day in May, seems a long way from the Caribbean, yet it is the Caribbean that Major Green wants to know about as he approaches the desk in 2006. He has recently retired from the Staffordshire Regiment and is intrigued by a story he heard some years ago at the Regimental Museum.

Many hundreds of soldiers visit Culloden every year, from all parts of the globe. Some come as part of organised group visits, while others, like Major Green, make private arrangements and come to undertake research. This can often be a mutually beneficial arrangement, as these private researchers have more often than not uncovered information that would not otherwise be readily available to us.

Major Green's visit proves to be of this variety. His regiment, The Staffords, were previously the 38th of Foot and known before that as Dalzell's. They were the regiment that the government sent out to the Caribbean in 1707 and left to languish there for 57 long years before they were brought home in 1764.

It was a posting known as 'the grave of English soldiers'. Over 10 per cent of the men died on the eight-week voyage out there, and most of the rest fell to a variety of diseases, or to drink. The seven years immediately prior to Culloden were fairly representative. Between 1738 and 1744, the regimental strength had been augmented by the draft of around 960 men. Even this wasn't enough to maintain numbers, however, as losses due to climate over those same years amounted to some 1,168 men.

This was the reason for Major Green's interest in Antigua. He had read that 250 Jacobite prisoners were ordered to be sent to Antigua in July 1746 in order to bolster Dalzell's declining 38th. Jamaica was also intended to receive 100 of these prisoners to bring Colonel Trelawney's 63rd back up to strength.

If the Caribbean was considered a bad posting for an average British soldier, it was even worse for the Jacobites, who were already weakened by wounds and deprivation. One man from Elgin, a thirty-six-year-old messenger called William Jack, wrote home reporting that after being kept on the prison ships for nearly nine months, he was one of only forty-nine survivors of the original 157 prisoners. He wrote the letter while still at Tilbury and was transported to Barbados later that same month. How many of his fellow forty-eight survivors were still alive after the next few months is unknown.

Not all prisoners that were transported were earmarked for military service; many were destined to be sold at their port of disembarkation. This was one way in which the transportation agents could make their profit.

One agent, Richard Gildart, wrote to the government in May 1747 seeking compensation for the loss of just such valuable merchandise. The story emerges that on the evening of 5 May, at Liverpool, he was loading Jacobite prisoners from jails in both Chester and Carlisle onto two ships – the *Johnson* and the *Gildart*. The prisoners were handcuffed together in pairs in a boat which was then towed out to the ships. When they came alongside the *Johnson*, the boat fouled her cable and capsized. As the men were manacled together in irons, they had little chance, and eight of them were drowned. These included Andrew Gibb, Charles Gordon, Coll MacDonald, John MacFarlane and James Mackay.

Richard Gildart appealed to the Treasury on the basis of an allegedly large cost, supplying 'Provisions, Bedding and Cabbins in the ship' for these men, and the fact that he would not now be able to realise £7 each for them on the other side of the Atlantic. Whether he ever received any compensation is not recorded within the Treasury Board Papers.

Liverpool was a common port of departure for such cargos of prisoners. Just three days after Gildart's disaster, another ship left the Mersey with 150 prisoners aboard, including 15 women. This was the *Veteran*, whose master John Ricky and her passengers were bound for Antigua, St Kitts and Jamaica. They included a portion of the total consignment of 250 men promised to Dalzell's Regiment.

Dalzell's were to be disappointed however; and Dalzell's disappointment was, in turn, due to a great turn of good fortune for the Jacobite prisoners. On 28 June 1747, about a day out from making landfall in Antigua, the *Veteran* was captured. Francis Hamilton, the merchant in charge of the prisoners on the *Veteran*, later swore to a St Christopher's Justice of the Peace that 'the said ship was attacked by a French Privateer Sloop called the *Diamond* of Martinique (Paul Marsal, Commander) and after a short engagement, was taken and carried into Martinique, and the prisoners there set at liberty by the Governour'.

The British Government was outraged, demanding the return of the prisoners from the French governor in Martinique. He understandably refused to take any action without instructions from France. The French Government, however, consistently refused to even consider the return of these prisoners.

The passengers of the *Veteran*, therefore, avoided the fate allotted to them when they left the Mersey and there appear to be no further references to them. However, we can surmise that a lucky few might have found their way home after the publication of the Act of Indemnity. It is likely that others made their way to France to join the regiments of past Jacobite Commanders, Lord Ogilvy and Lochiel, in the French Service. Some, like 'James Petrie' about whom an Alan Petrie first contacted the Staffords, may have settled permanently on Martinique – or is it just coincidence that there is an entry for Petrie in the Martinique Telephone Directory?

## New Lands, New Challenges

North American, and Caribbean, interest in Culloden is due to the histories carried by those who either emigrated, or were transported, to the New World. We have heard, too, about the French and Irish memorials upon the field, while French visitors are often already aware of the part their country played in the '45 rising.

Culloden tales have a far wider relevance than this, however. The battle was part of a larger struggle. The world was a deeply troubled place in the 1740s. The conflict that began on a snowy upland plain in Silesia in December 1740 involved only Prussia and Austria; that war, however, known as the War of the Austro-Hungarian Succession, spiralled quickly, drawing in almost every European State. It lasted for eight years and could reasonably be called a war of global proportions. At its height, the conflict stretched from the Ohio River in the West to Madras, India, in the East.

When the Jacobite rising of 1745 is viewed in the context of the wider military machinations, then it is easier to understand the involvement of German, Swiss, Dutch, French and Irish Regiments, fielded by one or other side, in Britain. The reasoning behind Louis XV of France's support for the Jacobite cause also becomes clear. The greater the number of British government regiments tied up at home on the British mainland dealing with 'domestic' issues, the better. That way, they could not be used against Louis in either Flanders or the North American theatre.

Nor were these the only countries with some degree of involvement. The Stuart 'palace in exile' was the Palazzo Muti in Rome, and the Pope, too, in the Vatican, had an interest in all these international manoeuvrings. The Spanish were far from neutral, providing the Stuarts with men and support, and Prince Charles's mother was the granddaughter of John Sobieski, the King of Poland. All in all, then, the '45 was far from a merely domestic squabble.

After the disaster at Culloden, many of the escapees made their way to the courts of European friends and supporters. France was the main destination but certainly not the only one. Many fleeing Jacobites also made their way to Norway and significant numbers of the men, particularly from Ogilvy's Regiment and Elcho's Lifeguards, made their way to Sweden.

The Schmidts were from Sweden. When they visited Culloden in early 2006, we quickly got into conversation about the connections between the two countries. We discussed the common cause, and intrigues, between James VIII and III, and Charles XII of Sweden. These kings had a shared enemy in Hanover: George I had occupied the Swedish outposts of Bremen and Verden and, from 1715, was using the British Navy against Sweden in the Baltic. By 1716, the Swedes were desperate and made direct overtures to the Jacobites in Paris.

The negotiations of 1716 and 1717 centred around the Jacobites lending a large sum of money to the Swedes; in return, a Swedish army, 10,000 strong, would invade England in support of a restoration of the House of Stuart. This plan suffered what could be described as a terminal setback with the death, in battle, of Charles XII in Norway in 1718.

Relations between Sweden and the Jacobites did remain warm, however; hence many escaping Jacobites tried to get to Sweden after the shocking, and sudden, defeat at Culloden.

'My neighbour, at home in Sweden, is descended from the Jacobites,' said Mr Schmidt. 'I wonder if you have any records of his ancestor here. The name is Ouchterlony.'

Well, I am ashamed to say that I had to confess to never having heard the name before. But I looked it up in a surname book, which suggested that the earliest known written reference to this family was recorded in 1296 and that the family originated in Angus. The name then spread up and down the east coast and different spellings developed.

I knew that many of the Lifeguards had been recruited in the eastern counties, and so I opened *No Quarter Given* at that regiment, before passing it to Mr Schmidt to check through. He was delighted when, on turning the page, the names of two Ouchterlonys seemed to leap out at him. John, an apprentice writer from Montrose, and Peter, a coffeehouse keeper from Dundee, were both in the Lifeguards and, as such, would have been at Culloden. We spoke for a while longer, then they left, taking with them all of the Ouchterlony details and leaving a promise, in return, that they would try to put their neighbour in touch with me.

Thomas Ouchterlony was good enough to contact me in October 2006 and he proceeded to round the tale off perfectly. He has correspondence from 1943 from Sir Thomas Innes, later Lord Lyon King of Arms. He stated: '*Ochtir* [meaning upper, or over] here refers to part of the Lownie area lying up-wards towards the Muir, or down across the ridge eastward to the burn of Latham.' The Ragman Roll, 1291–6, mentions, among the nobles of Angus, an Octirlowny of that ilk.

Thomas also recommended a book, *Scots in Sweden*, written by Jonas Berg and Bo Lagercrantz and published 1962, which tells of the escape after Culloden of Captain George Carnegie of the Lifeguards and an Ochterlony of Guynd. (The Guynd is a large house near Carnoustie – one of the ancestral seats of the

Ouchterlony family.) Together they fled into the hills, making first for Glenmark and Glenesk, and later escaping from the town of Montrose in an open boat. They were picked up by a Swedish ship and delivered safely to Gothenburg.

Thomas was very open, however, about the fact that any links between his own branch of the family, and those of the Guynd, were still unclear. What is clear, though, is that Thomas's family too appear to have been Jacobites. He explains that some family records suggest that his great-great-great-grandfather was Alexander, a merchant from Montrose, and an active Jacobite, who died on a political mission to Philadelphia in 1737. Alexander's father was the Jacobite Bishop Ouchterlony of Brechin, while his son is considered, by some, to be the best candidate to be the John (born 1729), who became a merchant captain, and, indeed, the ancestor who came to Sweden, and married a Swedish girl in Karlshamn in 1755.

The Ouchterlonys of Sweden all descend from John's son, Isaac, and have largely been civil servants, officers in the army or the navy, or academics. Thomas said that his great-aunt, Hanna Ouchterlony (1838–1924), was perhaps the best-known family member, a disciple of William Booth who introduced the Salvation Army into Sweden in 1882. In fact she was also the first leader of the Salvation Army in Sweden and then in Norway.

Thomas, himself, married a Scots girl and was for 25 years, until his retirement, director of the Council of Europe's office for liaison with the EU in Brussels.

This, then, is the crux of this tale. These are the ways that families, once Jacobite, spread out across the world, finding new directions and new ways of doing things. Some found new lives by active escape; others by the simple passage of time and of generations.

New lands and new challenges faced them all. They went on to become the citizens of many nations and to carry out the tasks associated with myriad different professions. Today, they speak in many different languages and represent a range of cultures and values. There are two things we can be fairly sure of, however: that a high proportion of them will eventually make their way to Culloden, and that more than a few of those will bring tales with them when they come to visit.

# PART FOUR

# TALES FROM THOSE WHO WORK ON THE MOOR

### Culloden

There was wind, there was rain, there was fire on their faces,
When the clans broke the bayonets and died on the guns,
And 'tis Honour that watches the desolate places
Where they sleep through the change of the snows and the
suns.

Where the graves of Clan Chattan are clustered together,
Where Macgillivray died by the Well of the Dead,
We stooped to the moorland and plucked the pale heather
That blooms where the hope of the Stuart was sped.

And a whisper awoke on the wilderness, sighing,
Like the voice of the heroes who battled in vain,
'Not for Tearlach alone the red claymore was plying,
But to bring back the old life that comes not again.'

    – Andrew Lang

# Register of Tales

## The Postie's Tale

Yes, I know that in today's politically correct society we are not supposed to call them 'posties' but that is what Susannah calls herself – and she is so good at her job and well liked by those on her round that I would not contradict her.

The fact that she often totes a 7-foot Lochaber axe, or a dirk and basket-hilted broadsword, on her time off might also have a bearing on not wanting to contradict her. Well, you wouldn't either, would you?

Our postie originally comes from Hanover, in Germany; however, her grandmother, who died when Susannah was four, was Scottish. Susannah grew up with an interest in thirteenth- and fourteenth-century history and became involved in setting up a re-enactment company which could portray this history for others, particularly the young. Then she left all that and came to Culloden, where, as a means of supporting herself, she took employment with the Royal Mail and became the postie for Balloch, on the downslope from the battlefield.

I asked her whether it was her grandmother's heritage that led her to Scotland.

'Not really,' she replied, 'but perhaps it was a slight factor in being drawn to find out about my roots.'

'What was it, then, that brought you here?' I asked.

'Oh, it's a strange story,' she said, 'but both powerful and true. I had a dream. I had it often. In the dream, I saw people running towards me. Falling down just in front of me. Cut down, and shot down. Dressed in colourful garb, the like of which I'd never seen before, and with such impressive weapons. I didn't know what any of it was about, but it was deep and disturbing. That is why I chose to go and speak to an interpreter of dreams.

'This dream interpreter asked if I could draw what I had seen. I said that of course I could. So this dreams professional consulted a history professor with the drawings, and he in turn shook his head and told me that what I had been drawing was a perfect example of an eighteenth-century Scottish Highlander. I couldn't believe it!'

That was the moment when she decided to dig into Scottish history and made the arrangements to come to Scotland to track down the Jacobites. It was inevitable that such a journey would ultimately bring her to Culloden Field. Almost immediately, she knew that she had a very special feeling for the place and she has, at the time of writing, been here for about eight years.

Susannah lives in a cottage on the edge of the moor. A visit there reveals a number of different talents. Outside the cottage, there is an impressive wood pile of chopped logs (although not, I think, hewn with the Lochaber axe). They have been stacked in the old way, with plenty of air channels to help with the drying. Inside the cottage, there are a number of different weapons and targes (clansmen's shields) in evidence and she is adept in all their uses. ('Why have them otherwise?' she says, with a shrug.) There are also some fine drawings hanging here and there. Some are complete, while others are works in progress. There are other ongoing projects evident, too, at varying stages of completion. Susannah makes facsimile weaponry out of wood and the end product, when painted, can look uncannily like the real thing.

Then there is the tartan. There are swathes of it, hanging, as if in tapestry, but actually ready for use. In fact, next time I meet her, she is wearing it.

'This is the old Highland battle gear of the mid-eighteenth century,' she tells me. 'My garb is the Feileadh Mor, or Great Plaid. It is about six metres long, woven of heavy Highland or island wool. To get dressed in it is a science in itself. The first thing is to lay it down flat on the ground. Then begin pulling the material towards you, folding it in a special way to form the pleats at the back of the

Feileadh Mor, getting all of this material behind you, out of the way, until you need it. Put your belt underneath, lie down on it and fix it around you. Then stand, dressed in your Great Plaid. It can be worn over the shoulders as a cape, or pinned up over one shoulder, but leaving the sword arm free. It could also be worn as a cloak and the extra pulled up as a hood. Another use is as a bedroll, and/or a lean-to [a crude tent]. When worn over the shoulder, these tucked places are pockets. Look!' As a way of demonstrating the usefulness of all of these folds, she promptly produced a bewildering array of dirks, as if by magic.

There are some particular places that affect Susannah more than others. While on the moor, she tells me the story of an officer of Lord Lovat's Fraser Regiment. 'This man, a certain John Fraser, also simply known as MacIver, was shot through the knee with a musket ball early in the battle. He survived the advance of the redcoats across the field but was robbed and stripped by the Campbells. He lay naked all night but next morning crawled down to a wood near Culloden House where eighteen other officers also hid. They were found later, taken down and thrown against a wall at Culloden House.'

I tell her that I've heard of this man. 'Wasn't he among those massacred at the Prisoners' Stone?' I ask.

'Yes, he was, but he was not counted among the dead,' she replies.

We take the walk down to the Prisoners' Stone, otherwise known as the Stone of the Massacre of the Officers. The stone is a huge boulder, now set fairly deeply in Culloden Woods, surrounded by firs and birches.

'It was on the Friday that an officer of the Duke of Cumberland's regiment, the Royal Scots, found them. They couldn't walk, so were tied with ropes, flung in a cart and brought here. They were carried to this place and told to prepare for death. Those who could kneel down did so and started their prayers, and after that were shot, in the chest, from only a few feet. Imagine those poor officers preparing themselves for death and looking up into the muzzles of those massive muskets.'

She hesitates, to collect herself, then continues. 'The shooting had a devastating effect but nevertheless one of the officers survived. It was MacIver. Though badly injured, having been shot in the chest, he was apparently still moving and so the officer ordered the troopers to smash his head. They bashed one eye out of him and broke his upper jaw and his chest bone. After this, he was left for dead.

'Fortunately, a young lord, Lord Boyd, while passing by found some mercy and managed to carry poor MacIver to a nearby corn kiln, where he could be hidden. MacIver, although never healed, was after some months able to get about again on his own, on crutches, and he survived many years.'

As we begin to move away, I notice the tribute ribbons tied around the nearby birch tree. These are, of course, Susannah's doing. The ribbons, she says, are like the small wreaths of fir and pine that she makes and leaves here. They help bring on a little bit of contemplation and show some deeply felt respect.

This one story touches Susannah profoundly. She feels as if it is so familiar to her, as though she knows it personally. Sometimes people ask her, 'Don't you feel scared, wandering and meandering through the battlefield and down through the woods to a place like this in the darkness, or even on a full moon? Aren't you afraid?' Her answer is clarion clear. 'I'm just not!'

She goes to the Prisoners' Stone and the battlefield as often as she can – whenever she has time off. She also says that the Culloden area is where her absolute heart is now and she does not want to stray too far away from the place.

## The Haggis Driver's Tale

Culloden is a favoured destination for many of the backpacker minibus tours to the north of Scotland. Regular arrivals include MacBackpackers and Haggis. One morning, early in 2006, one of the Haggis drivers approached the front desk. This was unusual in itself as these parties tend to pass quickly through the building, going straight out onto the field.

He introduced himself as Neil Matthew and asked, tentatively, whether there was anyone in the building who might remember a theft being foiled in August 1996, the 250th anniversary year, or alternatively was there any kind of a note to that effect anywhere in the museum room.

After asking around, I told him, regretfully, that no one remembered such a thing and so asked for more of the details so that we could rectify the situation. He was happy to tell the story, as he feels justifiably patriotic and very proud to have protected an important artefact at such a special place as Culloden.

'I was only 11 years old on the year of the 250th anniversary. Having recently studied the Jacobites as a school project, I had persuaded my parents to bring me to Culloden. While in the museum room, I noticed that a man had accessed one of the glass cabinets and now had a pistol in his hands.

'Being 11, I too was interested in the guns, so I crowded closer to get a better look. It was at this point that he put the pistol in his belt, pulled his jumper over it and left with two other men. Realising something suspicious was going on, I followed them as they headed for their car – a black VW Polo.

'I watched carefully, got all the details and then came back in to tell my father. He told the property manager, who in turn contacted the police. Shortly after, two policemen arrived at the visitor centre to take a statement. They brought news that, due to my actions, the trio had been caught in Inverness with the gun. My family were treated to a free lunch and I was also given a cash reward. I still remember all the details like it was only yesterday . . . even the car registration number!'

This is a story that connects Neil particularly and personally to the site. Now that he is a Haggis driver it is also a story that he takes great pleasure in recounting on every trip north. Thus it has become part of his working life and a part of the Culloden that he passes on to others.

## The Engineer's Tale

The summer of 2006 brought a man to Culloden who was in all ways down to earth, practical and no-nonsense. He was an engineer who had worked locally at Mid-Coul Farm in the 1960s. He wanted to know exactly where the road by the battlefield had run before its realignment in 1984. With a little extra encouragement, he also admitted why he was interested, although he was at pains to say he wanted to remain anonymous within the pages of this book.

In June 1963, he was staying at a pig farm in Croy. He and a milkmaid from Mid-Coul took a run to Culloden in his jeep at around 10.30 p.m. They parked by the clan graves and, with the jeep windows open, had a smoke. That was when they heard the sounds. Horses first, neighing and clip-clopping along, then people marching and mumbling. The noise grew and grew all around them to a crescendo, but with nothing to be seen. Scared witless, they tried to start the jeep. Nothing, not even a spark, despite it always having started before. Then, slowly, the noise faded. When all was quiet, the jeep started. The couple headed for Croy, with no delay and pounding hearts, and resolved not to talk of the occurrence to anyone, lest they be ridiculed. They kept silence for over four decades, until now, choosing to speak here.

# The Re-Enactor's Tale

You have met Duncan Cook before. He was my colleague involved in the story of the Night March told in Part Three. Duncan is a re-enactor, or first-person interpreter, at the visitor centre. He is, therefore, a number of different people while he is at work.

When we saw him before, he was Richard Cook, a soldier fighting with the Royal Ecossais, one of the regiments provided by King Louis XV of France. Richard Cook was a real soldier, a deserter from Howard's Regiment in the government army: then fighting for the Jacobites; later to be hung, in Inverness, for desertion and treason.

Sometimes, when Duncan takes tours round the field, he is Henderson, an eyewitness, an author and a biographer of the Duke of Cumberland. But when he performs the short dramatisation, 'A Day Like No Other', in Leanach Cottage, the old heather-thatched house that stands on the battlefield, he is Surgeon Grainger. This is his original, and perhaps most familiar, role. On the day of the battle, the real James Grainger was a surgeon's mate in Pulteney's Regiment.

The play in the cottage lasts only ten minutes but, in that time, poignantly examines both the tragedy of civil war and the role of the women who marched with the British Army in the eighteenth century.

The cottage is the ideal location, as records indicate that a couple of smallholdings, such as this, were used as military medical dressing stations for the government forces.

When asked if any particular stories or incidents characterise his time here, Duncan does not hesitate. 'Yes, it was in the first year of the play, about 1997. At that time, we kept all of the surgical and historical instruments in a large grey box. For security purposes, the box was locked up every night with a heavy-duty padlock and chain. The second interpreter, who took the part of Mistress Chisholm, was at that time a person called Cathy.

'Our habit, then, was for whichever of us arrived first to go out to the cottage, open up the box and take some time setting out the extensive array of instruments. I arrived on the particular morning in question to find Cathy already in. As usual, I checked with her as to whether she had opened and set everything up. "Yes," she said. "Everything's done." So, I trundled out, cottage-wards, with the Brown Bess Musket, the last of the props needed for the day.

'Imagine my annoyance when I discovered that the box was locked after all, and that nothing was ready. Time was ticking, and now we were behind schedule. I quickly went back to the centre for the key and more than tetchily told Cathy that she had not unlocked it at all that morning. She looked at me as if I was losing my marbles and insisted on accompanying me back out to the cottage with the key.

'You can't begin to picture how the hair stood up on the back of my neck as we re-entered the cottage, really only two or three minutes after I had left it, to find the box open, the chain and padlock neatly stowed away and all of the instruments perfectly laid out for the day's performances.'

'So, was that a one-off?' I ask. 'Or was there ever any kind of repeat performance?'

'It was the one and only occasion, thank goodness. I also have suspicions that to this day Cathy thinks I had some kind of mental aberration. I don't really know what to think. I do feel that something very strange occurred and I also know that whenever I think of that morning it gives me a slightly funny, uneasy feeling. But then that's just the kind of place this is, eh? It's a place full of echoes.'

# The Story of the Targe

The sun had not risen far above the surrounding hills. It was striking low through the trees and turning the thatched roof of the Highland Cottage buttermilk yellow. It was a morning with bite. As he prepared some feed for the livestock, John White could see the horse's breath, coming in starts and hanging in the still air, before them.

Then he went inside to get Ela. He warned her about the chill of the morning and so she went to get her heavy plaid to wrap around her body and her mob-cap for her head. She told him she would bring the weapons to the gate if he would just go and wait there for her.

As he waited, he let his mind run backwards to the fall of Carlisle. It was then that the elder John had been taken prisoner and shipped out to the New World. So much had happened since. He told the stories often, so that they would not be forgotten and the young people would carry them forward.

The sun was higher now and it was a bit warmer. Here was Ela, swathed in tartan and cradling the Swivel Gun in her arms. Yes, Swivel Gun! Ah, perhaps I neglected to mention that this Highland Cottage, surrounded by a comfortable framing of authentic outbuildings, was constructed by John, Ela and friends as part of the Ancient Lifeways Insititute in Michael, Illinois.

John and his wife utilise the historical and ancient worlds as a source of stories and learning to offer positive benefit to people in our busy twenty-first century. The institute specialises in the lore of the traditional North American tribal groups and more recently in the lore of the tribal clans of the eighteenth-century Scottish Highlands.

The Whites have spent their lives learning a better way to teach history, archaeology, anthropology and ethnography, the recording of human cultures. John is the director of education and worked for many years as an anthropologist at the nearby Kampsville

Archaeological Center. He believes that when people have the chance to practise the old skills they more deeply appreciate and understand the artefacts and the people. 'Living the experience' he feels also helps young people, in particular, to more readily understand the culture of our ancestors.

This particular day, in October 2002, John and Ela were out and about, taking photographs of their Tigh na Cailleach (the house of the old woman) so that they could send them to me at Culloden.

I had first met John and Ela when John had visited the battlefield the previous Easter. He came to undertake some Jacobite storytelling for the younger visitors, as part of the anniversary commemorations. I listened to his tales with a growing interest. As the days passed, we became friends and he told me the story of his own family.

It was not until the 1990s that the Whites first visited Culloden while searching for information about their Scottish roots. However, their interest intensified when a former property manager found out about their family connection to an ancestor who served in the Duke of Perth's Regiment.

This ancestor was also called John White, a labourer from Liberton in Midlothian. He served in Robert Taylor's company of the Duke of Perth's Regiment, which was part of the battalion that Prince Charles left at Carlisle when he marched back into Scotland on 20 December 1745.

As we read in 'Echoes from the Cathedral', Carlisle fell after a nine-day siege, on 30 December 1745. The city walls had been breached by the continuous cannon fire of the Hanoverian artillery and John White was amongst the hundreds taken prisoner.

The prisoners were kept in appalling circumstances, probably as a result of Cumberland's pique at not being able to put them all to death immediately. More than a quarter of these Jacobites soon died from starvation and the poor conditions, and over the following months many more were executed or transported. One arbitrary practice, which weighed cruelly on the prisoners, was the drawing of lots in order to determine which of them would face execution, which would be sent overseas as slave or indentured servant, and which might just be lucky enough to receive a pardon and return home.

Nearly a hundred of the prisoners were dragged to the English Gate of Carlisle that summer to be hanged, drawn and quartered – a common English sentence for treason. The heads of many were placed on pikes around the city gates, as a warning to any other would-be insurgents. John White was lucky. He was amidst a contingent of prisoners moved first to Chester, then on to London, and ultimately he was discharged.

He nevertheless felt the pressure to follow his transported companions overseas and so emigrated to America soon after. Like many Scots, he found much that was recognisable within the North American tribal traditions and married a woman of the Cherokee Nation. His descendants, therefore, were imbued with knowledge and respect for the traditions of two cultures; our modern-day John, in particular, had a thirst for the past.

After the first few fact-finding visits to Scotland, John and Ela decided to incorporate aspects of the tales and skills from eighteenth-century Scotland into the broad range of offerings available at the Ancient Lifeways Institute.

As a direct result of this burgeoning interest in the '45 rising, John began undertaking further research on the Internet. This led, in the spring of 2002, to his discovery that a targe (shield) allegedly used in the Battle of Culloden might be available for purchase.

Even the name comes from the Gaelic word for shield, *targaid*. It was circular, often 20 inches in circumference, and constructed from a couple of layers of oak wood. The grain of the wood was set to run at right angles in each layer of this stout oak heart – almost like an early laminate. The whole shield was then covered in leather (often cow or deer hide), then elaborately tooled or patterned, and studded with complex designs of nail heads and brass bosses. The central boss was often constructed so that it could hold a foot-long wickedly offensive spike. The leather straps that held the whole 5-pound shield onto the forearm left the hand free to wield an equally murderous-looking 18-inch knife called a dirk. The whole ensemble was a perfect counterpoint to the basket-hilted broadsword brandished in the clansman's other hand.

The particular targe that John was now trailing has an interesting pedigree in itself. It had been one of the prized possessions of millionaire collector and publishing magnate William Randolph Hearst. This newspaperman was the grandfather of Patty Hearst, notorious worldwide as the heiress who, in February 1974, at the age of 19, was kidnapped by the Symbionese Liberation Army. Within three months, she was helping them to rob banks. All told, she ran with them for about 18 months before her final arrest in 1975. It is said that she was suffering from an extreme case of Stockholm Syndrome, in which hostages sympathise with their captors.

She was given a severe custodial sentence, commuted by President Jimmy Carter, and was released from prison on 1 February 1979. She was granted a full pardon by President Bill Clinton on 20 January 2001, the final day of his presidency. By chance, it was later that same year that John White got wind of the possible sale of the targe originally owned by Patty's grandfather.

It turns out that some time after William Randolph Hearst's death in 1951 the targe was acquired by a Canadian collector. John approached the gentleman and managed to purchase the targe. His express intention was to return it to Culloden, where it was thought it had previously seen fierce action. 'We thought that it really belonged back at Culloden in the hands of the Scottish people,' said John, 'rather than in the hands of a private collector.

I feel that the targe's return to Culloden will reunite it with its owner, whom I am sure lies buried here.'

John generously decided to gift the targe, rather than loan it, and it was shipped to me during 2002. I arranged for the National Trust for Scotland curatorial staff to examine it and was delighted when they not only confirmed its authenticity but also put its construction date at around 1720. This gives strength to the idea that it was used at Culloden and increases the likelihood that John's strong intuition regarding the owner's final resting place is true.

*In memory of John White, died 2006*

# The Tale of the Skree
## From Mike, the Battlefield Guide

'The night I'm talking about was in the early 1990s. It was November and three of us were camping at Kings Stables. I was already employed as a battlefield guide by then, and my two compatriots were members of the White Cockade Society, formed to raise money for charity by recreating historical journeys. Furthermore, I think it's important to clarify that the reason we were out and walking on such a cold night is that we were on our way to the Culloden Moor Inn for a wee drink. I stress again we were on our way *to* a dram, not on the way home *after* one. Given how strange the night was about to become I think it's important to labour that point.'

Here, Mike pauses, not for effect but just to find the right words to describe the next part of the evening encounter. This is unusual, as he is not the sort of man to ever be at a loss for words.

Mike is an independent guide on the battlefield and his organisation, Alba Adventures, has provided services to the site for 21 years. The company provides both a syllabus-based experience for primary schools during term time and, in high summer, offers one-hour walking tours of the field to visitors in general. So Mike knows the field well and his profession ensures a fluency of delivery when speaking. It was interesting, therefore, to watch him struggling to frame the next part of his tale.

'There was a full moon as we walked across the moor, and just a hint of mist starting to form. Although the evening was cold, it was blessed by that winter's edge that makes you glad to be out, so we paused at the stone inscribed "The Field of the English".

'I was looking down the government lines when I saw it. I drew the attention of the others to what looked like a large, black, broken umbrella, straddling the path, close to the yellow flag. Imagine our surprise, therefore, when it stretched itself and arose from the ground, looking like nothing quite so much as a giant black bat. It creaked its way into the sky, although not far, and then, after hanging there for seconds, it disappeared. It didn't fly away. It just disappeared, vanishing before our eyes, like the picture on an old TV – phttttt! – into a flat line, then gone.

'To say we were surprised would be an understatement. For a few moments, we just stood there, mental vacuum and mental funk. Then, in a burst of one-upmanship, we all headed down the lines to investigate. There was nothing to be seen and, in a reasonably upset frame of mind, we got on with the rest of the night.

'Next morning, when I visited the property, I told the manager – Ross Mackenzie – of our encounter. With a cry, he tackled a tottering heap of documents and paperwork to triumphantly reappear brandishing an article that had, many years previously, been published in a reputable newspaper. He gave a copy of the article to me, telling me that I had been one of the unusual few to have seen the Skree of Culloden.'

Mike, looking relieved to have got that off his chest, then supplied me with the article concerning the Skree. It explained that before the battle there had appeared, above the terrified Jacobite soldiers, a monstrous apparition. It was a harpy-like creature, hovering overhead on 'black leathery wings' with 'burning red eyes' and the head of a man. Called the Skree, it might be considered a hallucination, if not for the fact that one of the eyewitnesses was Lord George Murray, a general renowned for his level-headedness. It is said that after Culloden, while on the run, he read the Bible for months on end.

Legend has it that the Skree appeared to herald ill omen for the House of Stuart on the field and the next day, following the defeat, the Skree vanished . . . never to be seen again.

Or did it?

## The White Cockader's Tale

Nowadays, Ian Deveney is an Alba Adventures guide on the battlefield. We will hear his tale as guide a little later. For now, I am going further back, to a tale that Ian tells from his time as a member of the White Cockade Society, formed in 1985, in time for the battle's 240th anniversary. Before long, it attracted a membership of over a hundred people, who began recreating events from the Jacobite period to educate and inform the public.

The 250th anniversary of the battle was in 1996 – a time important and solemn for many people from all walks of life. There had already been some unrest, vandalism and theft in the weeks running up to the anniversary and the National Trust for Scotland was determined that the commemoration events would not be marred by similar. There had been night movement on the field, with people stealing flags and even one of the cast-metal maps for the visually impaired.

After some consideration, the Trust asked the White Cockade to provide a security presence on the moor the night before the anniversary, as a precautionary deterrent to anyone with theft or damage in mind. Since 15 April 1996 was such a significant date, there was a good turnout of members. In fact, between the squad based at Leanach and that at Kings Stables, there was a force of about 16 to 20 Cockaders in total. Ian was with the contingent staying at Kings Stables, who, I am told, were well behaved and so had clear heads when the emergency radio call came through from the Leanach troop not long after midnight: 'There's someone on the field acting suspiciously, and they've stolen a flag!'

That was enough for Ian and companions; six of them set out into the darkness. They headed onto the field by way of the old forestry track and paused near the French Stone to listen and choose direction. It was completely silent. Almost too silent, as if the night itself was holding its breath. And then there was a sound, a very small sound – like that of the slightest twist of a foot on gravel.

Well, all six switched on their torches simultaneously and had, by sense of hearing, trained their beams on just the right spot. About 15 yards in front of them, held, like a butterfly on a spike, was a figure, outlined in all this sudden light, complete with a Jacobite flag tied around him.

All he could see was a flash of light and six furious, large, fully armed Jacobite warriors appearing around him. With a deathly wail, he dropped to his knees, hands on his head, convinced, in his drug-induced stupor, that his last moment had come.

He was taken to Kings Stables and the field was checked. Ironically, no flags were missing, so the flag he was sporting as a fashion item was obviously one he had stolen previously. The police were then called to deal with him. When they arrived, they discovered that they also required a dog handler, as the man had parked his car across the gateway with a very large and enthusiastic Alsatian inside. Eventually, the dog, too, was taken into custody, which meant the car could be moved to allow access to the crowds expected for the anniversary on the fast approaching morrow.

When the police checked the perpetrator's house on Loch Ness-side, they found all of the other items stolen from the field. It had been the work of this one individual, after all. The police even found the missing raised map for the visually impaired.

Ian himself spent the rest of the night in question wrapped in his plaid, sleeping, with a couple of mates, on the moor near the flagpoles. He awoke on the morning of the anniversary tired but very proud. Scottish history had always been a passion of his and so to safeguard a heritage site like Culloden on such an auspicious date was, for Ian, like living in, and making, history itself.

# The Tale of the Herd Laddie

Greg Dawson Allen conducts Storywalks around historic Inverness. He came up to Culloden Battlefield just before Christmas 2006 to provide an extra attraction for the visitors over two or three days. We fell to talking and exchanged a tale or two. Those short winter days, and darkening Solstice evenings, were made for the passing of stories, and one of his tales is well suited to this collection. It concerns Cumberland's troops on their way to Culloden. With Greg's agreement, I include it here, in his own words:

'Alexander Kinnaird was a herd laddie (or "hirdie") from a farm in Banffshire, overlooking the River Deveron, which separates the fishing villages of Doune (MacDuff) and Banff. His daily occupation in the fairmtoun, besides mucking out the byres, was to take the black Highland cattle down to the fields and look after them as they grazed on the lush grass by the banks of the river. When darkness was closing in, he would herd them back up the slopes to the byre and settle them down for the night.

'The lore of the countryside and its creatures, and overheard stories around the fire's ingle-neuk, were Alexander's education. He was handy, too, using local wood, his knife and his skill, whittling away his time looking after his master's cattle. For a lack of knowledge of counting, he carved a notch in his hirdie stick [used for prodding the beasts to move along] to keep count of the head of cattle – a notch for every cow. A notch with a cut at either end up and down distinguished the one with one horn up, the other down; a notch with cuts across meant the black one with the white nose; diagonal strokes distinguished the one with the hairy tail, and so forth. Therefore the cattle were recognised on his stick as a diary of duties. All could change if individual cows were bought or sold.

'Things did change, and in no small manner. At the time of this story, 9 April 1746, Alexander Kinnaird had, as usual, taken the cattle to the banks of the Deveron to graze. Unbeknown to him, the Duke of Cumberland was advancing his many regiments westwards to meet the Jacobite forces commanded by Prince Charles. To cross the River Deveron, Cumberland had to commandeer the boats from the port of Doune and his engineers organised a ferry service, transporting troops, cannon, horses and all the supplies needed to sustain a campaign to Inverness and the north.

'Watching all this activity, Alexander was mesmerised by the colours, all the hustle and bustle. He had never seen anything like this in his life before. This was never like the markets in Huntly or Keith. His wonderment distracted him so much that, until he was grabbed and dragged in front of an officer supervising the operations, he was unaware of redcoats coming up behind him.

'Alexander was interrogated as to his reasons for being at the riverbank: was he a Jacobite spy? Of all this, he honestly told the truth. He knew nothing; he was only a hirdie lad looking after his master's cattle. Of being a spy . . . well, he didn't even know what a spy was.

'Things may have been different but for a soldier who brought to the attention of the officer Alexander's hirdie stick. Curiously, he examined the strange carved notches and counted 12 – coincidentally the same number of boats being used to transfer the troops to and fro across the Deveron. This was evidence enough in a time fraught with an anxiety to end the Jacobite rising once and for all.

'The poor hirdie, Alexander, was taken to the old ruined church of Boyndie, outside Banff, and was hung from the roof tree, the beam which once supported the heather roof under which the God-fearing worshippers prayed for the House of Stuart. Around his neck was slung a crude notice, proclaiming, "Hung as a Jacobite spy".

'As often as I share this story, I think, in each telling, that the story of Alexander Kinnaird is a resurrection of his life: a plain hirdie lad who would otherwise have been trodden into the mires of regretfully forgotten history.'

## A Tale of Moorhen and Marshal

When things began to fall apart on the field at Culloden, they went to pieces remarkably fast. From the start, the cannon and the mortars chewed huge and bloody holes through Charles's clan regiments. Later, the Jacobite charge faltered under the Brown Bess musket fire and was ultimately broken by a combination of grapeshot, bayonets and enfilade musket fire.

The air was thick with gunpowder smoke and reeking with the smell of sulphur. The cries of the wounded and dying filled the air and the acrid, coppery smell of blood rose from the heather itself.

Those Jacobites who could, fled back westward, across the field, pursued by the vengeful government dragoons. After the initial shock at this sudden turn of events, Prince Charles was finally galvanised into action. He realised that if he, too, was to survive then he and his party must flee. They rode from the field in the early afternoon, heading fast downslope to the south-west, crossing the River Nairn at the ford of Faillie and passing the Clach an Airm shortly thereafter. They reached Gorthleck that evening and were entertained there by the chief of the Clan Fraser, Lord Lovat.

They decided, though, to move on almost immediately, having heard that there were dragoons in the area. Travelling through the night, they crossed the mountains and reached Invergarry Castle early the following morning.

Charles, together with three companions, spent the next few days travelling from there to Borrodale, near Arisaig. This marked the beginning of his time as a fugitive – the period through which legend and song describes him as 'the Bonnie Moorhen'. The detail of this period is well documented in the pages of other books (*The Prince in the Heather* by Eric Linklater being one). I intend, therefore, to paint his journey with only the broadest of brushstrokes.

It was from Borrodale that he took an open boat with five companions and seven boatmen and headed for the Outer Hebrides. They were hit, almost immediately, by a storm of monumental proportions, but Charles kept everyone's spirits up and they finally made landfall at Rossinish, just off Benbecula.

The party then made their way north in the hope of commandeering a seagoing vessel at Stornoway. The town was hostile to the Prince, however, and held against them, so they had eventually to return down the island chain to Benbecula. These waters were now being patrolled by large numbers of armed government ships and their voyage south was eventful, involving a sea chase and subsequent escape.

The Prince and his companions reached Coradale, in South Uist, on 14 May and stayed there for over three weeks. A story – amusing but untrue – is told that while they were there Charles heard that there was a £30,000 bounty for his capture. After a little thought, he offered in return a price of £30 for the person of George II. The reality is that while in camp at Kinlocheil the previous August, Charles had heard about the bounty on his head and, after consideration, required Murray of Broughton to write a proclamation offering the same sum for George II's capture.

On 5 June, news arrived that enemy troops were closing in, forcing the fugitives to take to the sea again. Days of hardship followed and the party felt it necessary to split up. Ultimately, on the night of 21 June, Prince Charles was taken north to Ormaclett in company with only Captain Felix O'Neil and one guide. This guide, known as Neil MacEachain, was to become one of Prince Charles's staunchest helpers throughout this time on the run. He is also central to this tale, as it reels out down through the years.

Neil was a schoolmaster in South Uist. Having been to the Scots College in Paris, he spoke French, which also helped the Prince in these difficult times. At Ormaclett, Charles was taken to meet one of Neil's relatives. This famous meeting between Charles and Flora MacDonald took place in a summer sheiling, where Flora was tending her brother's cattle. She agreed to help convey the Prince to the Isle of Skye and left to make arrangements.

A week later, Charles, dressed as an Irish maid (Betty Burke), was joined by Flora, and together with the faithful Neil MacEachain they sailed for Skye. Charles was keen to carry a pistol in his petticoats for defence, but Flora was adamant about the danger that this would represent if they were given a close search. To this he replied, with a chuckle, 'Indeed, Miss, if we shall happen to meet with any that will go so narrowly to work in searching as what you mean they will certainly discover me at any rate.' Flora, however, would not budge on the point and Charles had to content himself with a short, heavy cudgel instead. How ladylike!

They came eventually to Portree on 30 June and, in the early hours of the following morning, the Prince was taken on to the Isle of Raasay while Neil and Flora went elsewhere. The Prince then travelled from supporter to supporter, leaving the MacLeods of Raasay, staying briefly with the Mackinnons on Skye and finally returning to the mainland and the protection of MacDonald of Borrodale on 10 July.

The Prince's enemies were again closing in and Borrodale's son, sent out to reconnoitre, reported that he saw 'the whole coast surrounded by ships of war and tenders, and also the country, by other military forces'. Indeed, a line of camps and sentries had been set from the head of Loch Eil to the head of Loch Hourn.

Penned in, harried and hunted, the Prince's journey now more than ever became a deadly cat-and-mouse game until, finally, Charles passed silently between two guard posts, breaking through the cordon, in the early hours of 21 July. Three days later, he joined the 'famous' Glenmoriston men at Corriegoe Cave, north of Loch Cluanie. These eight men are worthy of their own tale, but it is sufficient here to say that after serving the House of Stuart on the field at Culloden, they were determined to resist Cumberland and the occupying forces. Their lives were filled with bravado and adventure, and on meeting with the Prince at their cave their oath was typically extravagant, yet heartfelt: 'that our backs should be to God and our faces to the Devil; that all the curses the scriptures did pronounce might come upon us and all our posterity if we do not stand firm to help the Prince in his greatest dangers'.

Charles was with this band of outlaws for some time, at first in Glenmoriston (where their cave was described as having 'the finest purling stream that could be, running by his bedside within the grotto, and where he was as comfortably lodged as if he had been in a Royal palace').

One other fugitive from the defeat at Culloden was said to be in Glenmoriston at this time. Roderick MacKenzie, an Edinburgh timber merchant, whose father was an Edinburgh goldsmith, had served with Lord Elcho's Lifeguards. Coincidentally, it had been noted that he was about the same age and of very similar looks to the Prince.

In late July, surprised by a redcoat patrol, he was overtaken while trying to escape. He drew his sword to defend himself. On being mortally wounded, he had the great presence of mind, and sense of loyalty, to call out, 'Alas! You have slain your Prince.'

With minds full of little but the thought of the £30,000 reward, the soldiers cut the head from brave Roderick's body and took it to Cumberland at Fort Augustus. MacDonald of Kingsburgh, imprisoned there, refused to positively identify the head and so the Duke of Cumberland took it to London. By the time the Prince's barber, Richard Morison, was summoned from Carlisle prison, the passage of time had decayed the trophy and identification was impossible.

If this story is true, then, by distracting Cumberland and the search parties for some weeks in this way, it is undeniable that Roderick's heroism helped to save his Prince's life.

The Glenmoriston men moved to Strathglass and then southwards to Loch Arkaig. Charles finally left them, at Achnacarry, in late August. MacDonell of Lochgarry and Lochiel's brother, Dr Archie Cameron, had arrived to take the Prince into Badenoch.

Badenoch was Cluny MacPherson's country and by 5 September the Prince was benefiting from MacPherson hospitality at Cluny's 'Cage' (a mountain hideaway) on Ben Alder. He stayed there, with Lochiel, Cluny, Lochgarry, Dr Cameron and others, until, hearing of the arrival of French ships on the west coast, they started for Borrodale on 13 September.

They came to the River Lochy after moonrise on 15 September. Cameron of Clunes met them with a boat from Loch Arkaig, which the Hanoverians hadn't burnt. Lochiel stated that the boat did not look safe, after which the night shaped as follows:

> 'I will cross first,' said Clunes, 'and show you the way.' Then, on reflection, he said, 'I have six bottles of brandy, and I believe all of you will be the better of a dram.' This brandy had been captured from Fort Augustus, where the enemy lay in garrison . . . Lochiel said, 'Will your Royal Highness take a dram, and that from Fort Augustus too?' Which

pleased the Prince much that he should have provisions from his enemies. He said, 'Come, let us have it.' Upon this, three of the bottles were drunk. Then they passed the River Lochy by three crossings, Clunes Cameron with a party first, followed by the Prince with followers, and finally Lochiel and others. In the third and last ferrying the crazy boat leaked so much that there would be four or five pints of water in the bottom of the boat and, in hurrying over, the three remaining bottles of brandy were all broke. When the Prince called for a dram it was told that the bottles were broke, and that the common boatmen had drunk all that was in the bottom of the boat as being a good punch, which made the fellows so merry that they made great diversion to the company as they marched along.

On 19 September, at Borrodale, the Prince and his followers were happily reunited with Neil MacEachain, and the whole party then embarked on board the ship *L'Heureux*, which finally weighed anchor and took the exiles safely to France.

In another century, and another country, we see north Cheshire at the end of the 1950s. The earliest memory of one young girl from there involved moving from a three-up two-down small terraced house into a company house. It was not much larger, but the really big improvement was that it had a plumbed-in bath, unlike the usual tin bath in the kitchen. As a result, there was suddenly no shortage of teenage girls queuing up to babysit the four children.

Carol was one of those children to be babysat and her reminiscences have a strong sense of place and time. Their street was long, the surface cobbled and the houses were built of red brick. All the doors were always open and it was years before she came to the realisation that the neighbours were not, in point of fact, her aunties and uncles.

When it came time for her to attend primary school, she did not have far to go. The Church of England school was only about six doors down. It was a large building on her side of the road about midway down the street. Each classroom had an open fire and was separated from its fellows by partition walls. When it came to assembly time, a remarkable transformation occurred. All the partitions were pushed back to create one large hall.

Her memories of the '60s comprise a montage of Formica tables, women in pinnies, *The Avengers* in black and white on the TV, beehives and Beatlemania. The '70s saw her completing her time at secondary school, and college thereafter.

The spring of 1980 was a time of change for Carol. She and her sister both felt it was time to change their jobs. Opening *The Lady* magazine at seasonal employment, they stuck a pin in the page and found themselves, in almost no time, working in Drumnadrochit.

All this was a far cry from life in the south, yet she loved it. She was married, for a time, to an Inverness man by the name of MacDonald and also became a mother. Time and tide rolled on and Carol finally began working at Culloden in the spring of 2005. It was some months later that I chose to tell her the tale of the Moorhen and the Marshal.

Neil MacEachain escaped to France along with Prince Charles and reverted to using his clan name of Neil MacDonald. He received, as a reward for services, a lieutenancy in the Regiment d'Albany and, later, in 1747, a commission in Ogilvy's Regiment. He retired on a pension in 1763 when the regiment disbanded and married soon after. Of four children, only one son and one daughter survived infancy. The son, Etienne MacDonald, joined a Dutch regiment in 1785 at the age of 20. Just three years later, in 1788, Bonnie Prince Charlie breathed his last. By coincidence, so did Etienne's father, Neil.

Etienne obtained a commission in the French Army and had,

by 1794, become the equivalent of a major general. Four years later, he was appointed as the first French governor of Rome. He was instrumental in defeating the Austrians at Wagram in 1809. To recognise this, Napoleon, there and then on the battlefield, made him a Marshal of France, an unusual honour, and also later created him Duke of Tarentum.

This seemed to be a suitable place to end the tale, with the bestowal of a title on this military son of Neil MacEachain. Or so I thought!

As I finished telling Carol this story, she exclaimed excitedly, 'But that's my brother-in-law's title! I never knew the significance or history behind it. I only knew that the title had come to him by virtue of his being a MacDonald, and resident in the same house in Boulogne as was a Marshal of France, called Etienne.'

So that, then, is the real end to this tale. Carol took the job on the front desk at Culloden with no knowledge whatsoever of any personal links with the site. She was just a lass from north Cheshire who had, at one time, been married to a MacDonald. Yet, following the revelation of the history behind the title the Duke of Tarentum, it is clear to her that a direct connection exists between her family and one of France's greatest military heroes, and this consequently also highlights a link to one of the Prince's most loyal supporters, Neil MacEachain.

It also underlines, for me, one unusual aspect to Culloden Battlefield. It is the kind of place where stories collide.

## The Storyteller's Tale

The role of the storyteller, the *Seanachaidh*, here at Culloden is essential for both the giving and receiving of tales. There is a need, in such places, for someone who sees it as important to learn the stories – old and new – and who can choose which stories to tell, to which visitors, in order to make the very ground sing and the place have proper meaning and significance. I do not know how often, or if ever, I manage to do that, but I try. I do that because I feel that I owe it to the distinguished storytelling family that I follow on the battlefield.

Mrs Annabell Cameron (née Bell MacDonald) was the last inhabitant of Leanach Cottage, the last of her line to guide people around the moor. She was long-lived and a battlefield guide most of her days. Leanach Cottage was left empty after Bell died in 1912, aged approximately 83 years.

Her father, James MacDonald (of Leanach), was a guide on the field before her and was the man called upon in 1846 to guide notable visitors around the moor on the 100th anniversary of the battle. A decade earlier, in 1835, when a new road was driven through the graves, it was said in a local journal: 'James MacDonald, however, who lived in the old house of Leanach and saw the work done, said the bones had all been re-interred.'

Bell's grandfather, also James MacDonald (but of Culchunaig), was an even earlier guide (sometimes described by the old term 'local cicerone'). The mother of that older James MacDonald was still living with her parents at Culchunaig in 1746. She was baking on the day of the battle when a Highlander who had lost his hand rushed in and cauterised the bleeding stump by pressing it on the hot stones of the fireplace.

These five generations have done an excellent job in setting the standard (to which I have continually aspired) for storytellers on the site.

## Forbes of Culloden – A Family Tale

Janet Honnor is a frequent visitor to the battlefield. She is a local independent guide and so Culloden is a regular work-stop for her. But it is also far more than that, for Janet is bound to these acres by ties of both blood and heritage. Her mother was a Forbes and she herself is the granddaughter of Hector Forbes, 13th Laird of Culloden, the man who gifted Leanach Cottage, Kingstables Cottage, the clan graves and the Memorial Cairn to the National Trust for Scotland in 1944. Janet's brother, Duncan, is now the 15th Laird of Culloden.

The family heritage is recorded back through many centuries, flowing from the ancient families of Forbes of Tolquhon, and Keith, Earl Marischal. As a young child, Janet lived in her grandparents' house, Ryefield, on the Ferintosh Estate. Family portraits hung on the walls and each face was connected with some incident in Highland history, recounted by her grandfather with great pride. Janet now takes great pleasure in telling these same stories for the enlightenment of any visitors to the area.

'Our family became owners of Drummossie Moor when an early Duncan Forbes, Member of Parliament and Provost of Inverness, purchased the Mackintosh Estate of Culloden in 1626, so becoming the first Forbes of Culloden. He was the bearded, formidable-looking individual whose portrait can be seen, to this day, hanging in the main chamber of the Townhouse in Inverness. He lived a long and productive life, dying in 1654, aged 82.

'His son, John, was also Provost of Inverness and became the trusted friend and supporter of the Marquis of Argyll. This strong support of Protestant Presbyterian principles meant that he suffered much in the times of Charles I, the Ferintosh Estate being rampaged over by Montrose's men.

'The next laird was John's son, Duncan (3rd of Culloden), and his staunch Protestantism led him to support William of Orange, both in 1688 and through the troubles of 1689. The losses that the Forbeses suffered in this revolution were compensated in a unique way by the Scots Parliament. They were awarded the privilege of distilling into spirits the grain of the barony of Ferintosh at a nominal and set level of duty, price-protected at a time when spirits in other parts of the country were subjected to both heavy, and increasing, excise charges. The government later realised the value of the privilege and insisted on buying it back. Duncan had two sons, John and Duncan, and several daughters.

'Our family supported the Hanoverian regime from the time of their succession, and John (4th of Culloden) was also active in their service during the '15. He narrowly escaped capture by the Jacobites at Aberdeen and subsequently went on to suppress the troubles in Inverness-shire. His younger brother, Duncan, was destined for even greater things. He was born in 1685 and educated in Inverness, Edinburgh and Leyden. He was admitted to the Faculty of Advocates in 1709, at the age of 24. Both brothers were renowned for their hospitality and hard drinking, as Burt described in his *Letters from a Gentleman in the North of Scotland* after dining at Culloden House. But they were also firmly instilled with their mother's work ethic and Calvinist principles. She writes to Duncan, at one point, to say she was "much surprised and grieved to find he had journeyed from Innes on the Sabbath".

'Duncan became the 5th Laird of Culloden in 1734 (inheriting from his childless brother, John). He was Lord Advocate and Lord President of the Court of Session, and MP for Inverness, Nairn and Forres. The family had personal links with the Duke of Argyll, with whom he worked closely during his political career. He worked tirelessly throughout his life to support and help Scotland and the Highlands.

'It is interesting to note Duncan's wide net of kinship (which in those days was of great importance – and still mattered much when I was a child) and friendships that emerge through his letters. These were written to people throughout Scotland, both to those who supported the House of Hanover and those who supported the House of Stuart – sometimes these were even in the same family. The general confusion of war comes across with great immediacy in these letters, as do the difficulties associated with communication and provisions for troops in an area where supplies were scarce and conscript soldiers on both sides were likely to melt away into the hills.

'His correspondence was as awesome and continuous as his travelling. He frequently undertook the return journey between Edinburgh and London, and covered most of Scotland in an effort to persuade his countrymen of the benefit and wisdom of supporting the Government. He was well liked and respected by his fellow men, many of whom took his advice.

'Duncan escaped Inverness just hours before the Jacobites' arrival on 18 February. He went first to Sutherland, then later to Skye. His home at Culloden was occupied by Prince Charles before the battle and by Cumberland afterwards. The Lord President was able to return to his own house on 22 April 1746, barely a week after the battle, which had, of course, been fought on his land.

'Trying to limit the damage to the Highlands in the aftermath of Culloden was difficult. The Lord President's view was clear: "No severity that is necessary ought to be dispensed with: the omitting of such severity is cruelty to the kingdom. But unnecessary severities only create pity, the nurse of disaffection."

'Duncan became ill the following year. I was told as a child that he was worn out with his work for the government and the Crown. He had been required to use his diplomatic skills and local knowledge almost ceaselessly to petition on behalf of those wrongfully imprisoned, seeking their release. The brutality of the aftermath of Culloden was said to have broken his heart, not to mention the lack of reimbursement from the government and the expenditure of his own money to pay the armies to save the Kingdom. After great hassle, he was repaid a third of the amount. Worst of all, there was no acknowledgement of his great loyalty, integrity and wisdom over many years on the Crown's behalf. He died on Thursday, 10 November 1747.'

Janet pauses reflectively, thinking again of the life and times of this illustrious ancestor, before going on to bring the story more up to date.

'My own first visit to Culloden was as a child of ten. I was shown the gun-ports, and the cellars where Forbes' steward hid 18 Jacobite prisoners after the battle. At the time of the battle, of course, Culloden was a barmekan fortified house [one with defensive cattle enclosures, typically Scottish] and not the Georgian house you see today. The present structure was built after the original building caught fire in 1757 and nowadays has been converted to serve as the luxury Culloden House Hotel.

'During the same visit, on a hot summer day, we rode our ponies up through the pine-scented forest, past the Lord President's Seat – a large boulder so called as it was one of his favourite spots. We carried on, to the prehistoric Cloutie Well, where we stopped to drink and then finally we ventured on up to the old road and the clan graves, at that time surrounded by forest. My companions told me about this being the site of the last battle fought on British soil and the terrible death toll of the Highlanders. I felt guilty about my family being on the other side! I was also shown the great 20-foot Memorial Cairn, raised in 1881 by my grandfather's great-uncle, the 10th Laird (also called Duncan).

'Many years passed before I visited the site again. My husband was in the Royal Navy and we lived in Devon. On his retiral, however, my mother gave us a plot upon which to build a house only one mile from the battlefield. For many years, I walked my dog around the site in wind and rain, and sun and snow, both by day and by night. I remember one particularly magical night when it was both snow-covered and lying under a full moon – a combination that was breathtaking. In springtime it was flooded in larksong and wildflowers. At no time was I ever troubled with ghosts or spooks, but there was one curious incident, involving my son.

'Patrick was seven. We had friends staying. That morning we had had a problem finding where our water main joined and they suggested we make divining rods with wire coat hangers. You balance them on your fingers so they face straight ahead and when they locate water they cross each other in the middle. They worked perfectly, pinpointing the water main in no time. Patrick took them with us when we took our friends to walk the battlefield. They crossed over at the Well of the Dead and various water sources. Then he leapt onto one of the burial mounds and, to our astonishment, they swung *outwards*! Our friend said that this is what happened when bones were underneath. There had been a rumour, at that time, that the battle had been fought closer to Culloden House, but this incident convinced me that the present site is correct.'

Janet ended there, having said enough about both her forebear, the Lord President (5th of Culloden) and her own relationship with the battlefield over the years.

Blood and heritage are, as previously mentioned, the ties which connect Janet to this field and, before we finish our tale, it would repay us to revisit her grandfather's great-uncle, Duncan, 10th Laird of Culloden, who, as we have already heard, is the man responsible for building the cairn and erecting the other memorials on the field in 1881.

Like so many representatives of this family, Duncan (the Memorialist) obviously felt very deeply about the moor and the tragedy that unfolded upon it. I believe that Duncan would have been well pleased with Janet's grandfather's decision to donate the memorials to the National Trust for Scotland. The NTS is a conservation charity and, in his day, Duncan was very much an early leader in the field of conservation. He was intensely interested in all of the historic sites that abound within the surrounding area. One report of him notes: 'Mr Forbes of Culloden gave a good example to other proprietors, in having a clause inserted in his leases binding the tenants to preserve all such monuments of antiquity.'

The Memorial Cairn which he personally financed, and caused to be raised next to the clan graves, carries the inscription:

THE BATTLE OF CULLODEN
WAS FOUGHT ON THIS MOOR
*16th April, 1746*
THE GRAVES OF THE GALLANT HIGHLANDERS
WHO FOUGHT FOR
SCOTLAND AND PRINCE CHARLIE
ARE MARKED BY THE NAMES OF THEIR CLANS

This inscription is nowadays considered a bit narrow, as it recognises neither the civil war aspect of the strife nor the composition of the armies. It is, however, a fine memorial built with good intentions and serves well in remembrance of *all* of the fallen.

It is therefore fitting that, upon his death in 1897, Duncan's own obituary was also a fine individual memorial:

> His heart was so kind, and his disposition so amiable, that he could bear no malice or ill-will towards anyone. It goes without saying that he was universally esteemed by all classes of the people.

# The Tale of the Disappearing Stone
## From Ian, the Battlefield Guide

Following on from the previous tale, which included information on the placement of all of the memorials and gravestones on the field, it seems appropriate to mention 'the one that got away'.

Ian Deveney (first heard of here in relation to the foiling of the flag theft) tells a strangely believable story about a disappearing stone. He and a friend called Martin were walking the Jacobite line on the field one year, around anniversary time. They were having a more in-depth than usual poke around the right wing and crossed the fence into the Field of the English. They headed close to the

Culchunaig boundary and, hard up against a hedge, they came upon a very old stone.

This stone was very much of the same vintage, size and type as the clan gravestones. It was 2½ to 3 feet high, and although it had its back against the hedge, there were, nonetheless, worn trackways in the grass leading to it from the other three sides. It seemed to them to be another grave marker – despite it having no plaque and no significance that they knew of.

They headed back to the visitor centre to ask for more detail from the two men most likely to know: Ross Mackenzie, the property manager at the time, and Mike Newcomen, proprietor of Alba Adventures. Neither of them had ever heard of, or seen, such a stone, so Ian and Martin took Mike out to show him where it was located.

They went by exactly the same route, but there was no stone to be seen. They did not believe the evidence of their own eyes and so looked everywhere. But the stone had disappeared; even the track marks in the grass had gone.

Despite taking a job at Culloden as a battlefield guide from 1998 onwards, and looking often in the intervening eight years, Ian never saw that stone again.

## Heirs and Graces

A claim to the throne of Britain, or provable descent from one of the most romantic Princes in European history – these represent powerful possibilities. Some people might find those ideas intriguingly seductive, while others are genuinely appalled at even such a whisper; fearful of being labelled deluded or self-serving.

Many individuals throughout history have made such claims, usually with no evidence and even less reason. There are others, however, who bring tales worth telling. I will relate four of them here. The people in the first three stories have all had a relationship with Drummossie Moor in some capacity at one time.

## The Sobieski Stuarts

These two brothers claimed to be grandsons of Bonnie Prince Charlie and his 'Queen', Louise of Stolberg. They averred that their father, a Thomas Allen, had been born in 1773 and delivered into the safe hands of Admiral Allen, who spirited the baby out of Italy and raised him as his own. This Thomas Allen assumed the title 'Count of Albany' and lived quietly until his death in 1852. His sons, however, were striking society figures who went by the names John Sobieski Stolberg Stuart and Charles Edward Sobieski Stuart. The most ardent supporter of their claims was Monsieur le Vicomte d'Arlincourt, in his book, *The Three Kingdoms*, published in 1844. They were also recognised by the Lord Lovat of the day, who provided them with a house at Eilean Aigas, an island on the River Beauly. It was from here that they made trips around Inverness-shire and to Drummossie Moor.

The Sobieski Stuart claims were never verified – no valid documentation was ever found (even by d'Arlincourt) – and neither Prince Charles nor Louise ever mentioned any issue of their union. If the claim was genuine, then the British Intelligence Service would surely have known of the birth of such a child (which they did not) and Charles would also undeniably have acknowledged any legitimate male heir in 1783, instead of recognising Charlotte, his daughter by his mistress Clementina Walkinshaw.

Even though the Sobieski Stuart claim was patently false, they were, nonetheless, charismatic and colourful characters in their own right. As well as being handsomely adorned in Highland dress, they owned many objects from the Jacobite period. They were also accomplished writers; Andrew Lang describes their *Lays of the Deer Forest* as an excellently written natural history. The elder brother, John, wrote *Vestiarium Scoticum*, published in 1842, and *The*

*Costume of the Clans* in 1845. These works were long considered the standard authority on tartans and Highland dress.

John died suddenly on board a steamer just leaving Bordeaux in 1872 and Charles Edward on Christmas Eve, 1880. They were both buried beneath large Celtic crosses in the beautiful little churchyard of Eskadale, by their beloved River Beauly.

Sir Walter Scott said that their claims arose from 'an over-indulged habit of romantic day-dreaming' while Andrew Lang thought that they 'acquired the force of an actual hallucination'. J. Cuthbert Hadden says, in his book, *Prince Charles Edward*:

> The brothers had a touching and an absolutely sincere belief in their connection with the fallen house of Stuart; and the fact that they went through life accepted by a vast number of people as the grandsons of Prince Charlie, seems sufficient reason for giving them once more a place on the borders of the living land.

## HRH Prince Michael Stewart of Albany/Michel Roger Lafosse

I first met the man who claims to be Michael Stewart (a direct descendant of Prince Charles Edward Stuart) at the Culloden Anniversary Service in 2001. He attended the service every year from then until 2006 and generally arrived amidst a flurry of pomp and circumstance – flags, bodyguards, adherents and a political wing.

The property manager at that time, a renowned Jacobite scholar, would not let this party into the building. He said that he had undertaken extensive personal research – including time spent at the archives in Rome – and had not found one piece of evidence that would reinforce any of the claims made by the alleged Prince Michael of Albany.

Michael's main claim is that Bonnie Prince Charlie, after a secret papal annulment of his first marriage, became secretly married a second time. Michael says that this union produced an heir in 1786,

Edward James Stuart, Count Stuarton, Count of Albany. Michael claims direct descent, and title, from this person.

As with the Sobieski Stuarts, no valid documentation has ever been produced to back up these claims and, except for Michael's own version of events, the Jacobite historians and scholars that I know have never heard of either a second marriage or an Edward James Stuart, Count of Albany.

Michael was born in Belgium in 1958 but left as soon as he could, arriving in Scotland in the late 1970s. His claims ensured that he soon attracted a following and his political wing was soon known as the 'Loyal Men'. He wrote a book, published in 1998, called *The Forgotten Monarchy of Scotland*, which contained a history of Scotland and the case for his relationship to the House of Stuart.

There has been media interest in the Michael Stewart story from the outset, but this intensified with the announcement by Scottish genealogist Gordon MacGregor that he had uncovered documents which call Michael's claims into question.

There was a major investigative article by editor Neil Mackay in the *Sunday Herald* on 2 April 2006 which, as well as reporting that Belgian officials had pronounced his birth certificate to be false, identified Michael as Michel Roger Lafosse. The article also highlighted other areas of concern regarding Michael's certificate of naturalisation and the passport which he uses for diplomatic travel.

My last encounter with Michael was at the 2006 anniversary service, for which he arrived quietly, both late and alone, and walked quickly out to the main Memorial Cairn.

By June, two articles, by Norman Silvester of the *Sunday Mail*, were published. The first reported that Michael was set to be deported after having lost British citizenship because, it is alleged, he submitted a forged birth certificate. The second told how, following the loss of his citizenship, he had sold up his house in Edinburgh and returned to Belgium to live with his mother.

Reading these articles, I did feel moved by Michael's somewhat tragic fall from grace and was very powerfully reminded of the words of Sir Walter Scott, quoted earlier in reference to the Sobieski Stuart brothers.

## Peter Pininski

Prince Charles's daughter, Charlotte, had a long, covert relationship with Ferdinand de Rohan. Their relationship developed in secret due to Ferdinand's position as Archbishop of Cambrai but also because of Charlotte's position, and her father's hopes of securing a Stuart future by arranging a political marriage for her. It did eventually become known that Charlotte had borne Ferdinand two daughters and a son, but it was generally believed that they had all died childless.

Count Peter Pininski was brought up in England by a Polish father and a Scottish mother descended from the Camerons of Lochiel. The death of Peter's paternal grandmother was the catalyst that spurred him to study Polish and learn about the country's culture and history. After the fall of communism, he began a new life in Warsaw as a historian and began a quest to answer a family puzzle.

It was while researching his mother's Cameron background, and their part in the '45, that he learned of the liaison between Charlotte and Ferdinand de Rohan. This interested him, as his family had always known that Peter's great-great-great-great-grandmother was a natural daughter of one of the Princes de Rohan. He then began to wonder how closely these two de Rohans might have been related.

The records of Peter's family had been lost, however, when their castle was plundered by Russians during the First World War. All that remained was an intriguing pastel portrait of the smiling young woman in question. Peter was determined to find out more.

This long and fascinating search is described in his book, *The Stuarts' Last Secret*, which tells how, twenty-two archives and seven countries later, he found baptism, marriage and death certificates, diaries, journals and letters which showed the smiling woman to be Marie-Victoire. Research had provided evidence that the de Rohan princes in question were not just related, they were indeed one and the same person!

Marie-Victoire, although raised and recognised by her uncle, was one of the two daughters borne by Charlotte to Ferdinand de Rohan and so was granddaughter to Prince Charles. This was completely unexpected and not the outcome Peter had foreseen when he first began his search. It is one reason why his findings are so believable. He had not sought to manufacture this connection but had instead stumbled across it by accident. His research methods are impeccable, the documents are genuine and his findings were even accepted by the chairman of the Royal Stuart Society in 2002.

Marie-Victoire, and indeed the generations that followed on from her son, are the 'Last Secret' that Peter writes of. However, he has always made clear his desire to completely avoid 'Stuart claimant-type charlatanism'. His motivations have always been simpler than that: a quest for historical information; a desire to find out more about the mysterious woman in the portrait; and a wish to leave a fuller understanding of family heritage behind for his own children.

### Franz, Duke of Bavaria/Francis II

If not Peter Pininski, then who, in the eyes of entrenched Jacobites, could be viewed as the *de jure* (lawful) heir to the throne of Britain?

Prince Charles Edward Stewart, known by Jacobites as King Charles III, died without producing a legitimate heir in 1788. His brother, Cardinal Henry, was then recognised as Henry IX and I. He died childless in 1807. This extinguished the legitimate line from James VII and II. There was then only one remaining line that could trace descent from Charles I: the family of his daughter, Henrietta.

Henrietta's great-great-grandson, Charles, King of Sardinia, was confirmed by Henry IX and I's will and he was henceforth recognised by the Jacobites as King Charles IV. His brother, Victor, succeeded him in 1819 and from there the succession descends in straight-line fashion.

Victor's great-granddaughter, Mary, became Queen Consort of Bavaria. Her son, the Crown Prince Rupert, temporarily went to Florence in Italy in 1939, seeking asylum from the Nazis. In 1996, Rupert's grandson, Franz von Wittelsbach, became known as Duke of Bavaria upon the death of his father. Those ardent Jacobites still seeking a monarch who can claim legitimate descent directly from Charles I recognise Duke Franz as Francis II.

There is no record of Duke Franz having visited Culloden Battlefield but, then again, his descent from Charles I links him more closely to the religious wars of the mid-seventeenth century – perhaps those battlefields sing a louder siren song to him than Culloden does.

## The Tale of MacFarlanes' Company

The descendants of the Jacobite rank and file, of course, far outnumber those whose ancestors may be identified as Stuart nobility. The descendants of Jacobite soldiers, prisoners, fugitives and sympathisers are scattered to the four corners of the earth. Many of the tales recounted in Part Three are from families of emigrants such as these. However, when seeking stories from people who work on the moor, I thought that Elliot MacFarlane was perhaps best placed to tell us what Culloden means to descendants living in North America – descendants like him and the members of his MacFarlanes' Company.

MacFarlanes' Company is a living history troupe of re-enactors from North America who are passionately committed to their rich

Scottish heritage. I have shared time and tales with them on many occasions now and include three of Elliot's best here. They are a trio of stories in his own words, contemplating the issue of connection to the field. The first tale explains the ties that bind Elliot and the others to this place. The second shows us that those same ties run through our lives, too. The third and final one reminds us that those who fell in the course of the battle have the strongest connection of all and will not be forgotten.

## Two Brothers

'Working in the cottage at the Culloden visitor centre seemed natural to us. From the company's first trip to the battlefield, we felt drawn to the cottage for presentations. We had all done years of living history, much of it at historical sites, but we felt most at ease working at the battlefield.

'It was inside the cottage on a raw April morning that we first had to address "the Question". We really didn't prepare an answer, although we knew it would be needed soon after we started to speak and our accents gave us away. "What do a bunch of guys from Canada and the United States know about Scottish history, and what gives you the right to present it?" Two questions really, but closely related.

'The first part of the Question is the easiest to answer. We had made some of the best-researched presentations by living history re-enactors and we had been doing them for years. I had been working on the details of our trip for quite some time and had come over the previous year to finalise the project with National Trust staff. I had been charged by the NTS to bring the best Scottish-costumed historians I could find in North America. Each member of the group had a long history of research and living history behind them. All were well studied, specifically in eighteenth-century Scottish history.

'To the "What do a bunch of guys from Canada and the United States know about Scottish history?" part of the Question, there was a straightforward answer: we knew what the people in Scotland knew about the eighteenth century because we learned it the same way.

'It may seem that the answer to the second part of the Question should have been as obvious; we have the right to present it because we know what we are talking about. But this answer would not have made us any friends and, more importantly, it did not get to the intent of the question. What we were really going to be asked was "How do you presume to tell US about OUR history?"

'I had finished a somewhat animated description of what had taken place at the site and was showing swords to a 12 year old when the Question came. I begged off from answering and told a story instead.

'Imagine, if you would, two brothers standing in the ranks on 16 April 1746. The snow in their faces and their swords in hand, they prepare to charge toward the Hanoverian guns. Not so very much later they come back, separated in the smoke and carnage. In the chaos and confusion, the two are lost from one another.

'One brother flees to France and one, captured, is shipped across the Atlantic. The sons and grandsons of the brother in France come back to Scotland and live not all that far from where their grandfather tended cattle. The sons and grandsons of the other brother stay in North America.

'Now, let us look around this cottage and see the great-great-great-grandsons of each. Does one of those grandsons have the right to present the history of his ancestor and the other one not? Is it not the history of us all?

'Standing in the dim cottage, the sharp wind rattling in the thatch, not much else was said. As the group of visitors took turns ducking to clear the door, one man, ramrod straight and heavy

197

with white hair, stopped and offered his hand. "Welcome home," he said in the accent I so clearly lacked. "We missed you." There is much warmth in those old stones.'

## Bringing the Supper

'We were in the parking lot of the visitor centre one evening, packing up from the day's activities, when a small boy appeared beside the bus. His family was unloading from a car near us and he came over to look at the guns and swords and knives. This is not uncommon for us, as all boys are drawn to the weapons. Yet this young man was more interested in our names than our hardware. When we told him who we were, he seemed disappointed and told us directly, and with some regret, that he was not related to us. Soon, his sister arrived and wanted to know about us as well. After we explained who we were, her little brother told her we were not related to them. She told us why they were there so late in the day.

'The two had come to Culloden Moor with their grandmother and mother. Their grandmother brought them there a few times a year from their home near Fort William. Grandmother always brought a supper with them, which they ate during their visit. She had told the children that she liked to bring her family to Culloden in order to have supper with her relatives.

'As grandmother and mother arrived to retrieve the two, we got a clearer picture of why they were there and why it was so important to the young man to know who we were. Grandmother was a MacDonald and had ancestors buried on the battlefield. *These* were the relatives that she would come and eat her carefully prepared supper with at Culloden, as they patently could not come to her house! The boy knew his grandmother was old – and we certainly looked like we were old – and as he had never actually seen the relatives they came to eat with on any previous trip, we might just be them!

'As the lines were drawn up for battle on Culloden Moor, the MacDonalds were moved to the left of the front line. The Duke of Perth commanded that part of the line and, knowing the MacDonalds to be unhappy with their position, pledged to change his name to MacDonald if they would but follow him into battle. Had it been possible, I would have changed my name to MacDonald that evening. As it was, I had a ham sandwich with their relatives.'

## Midnight at Culloden

'We had arrived at Culloden in the late afternoon of a cold April day in 2003. Later, we went into town to attend the book signing and launch of Dr Duffy's new book on the Jacobite rebellion. Thus started an interesting evening.

'The book launch went well, after which we departed the shop and were standing on the street wondering where eight guys might buy a bottle of whisky on an Inverness Friday night. We returned to the bookstore to ask about a whisky shop and the store manager looked up smiling, as if expecting us. "I knew you would be back," he said. "I have whisky for you."

'We were surprised, to say the least, as he handed us two bottles, adding, "Share the spirits." At least I thought he said that. One of my mates thought he said "Share with the spirits." As we were to learn, there is a distinct difference.

'We had previously made arrangements to return to the battlefield that evening and look over the ground as it would have been on the eve of the battle. We wanted to see the ground as it was when thousands of men lay wrapped in their kilts, exhausted from the night march to Nairn, trying to get some sleep. We parked our van in the car park and trekked off toward the Jacobite end of the battlefield. We were some way across the moor when I remembered the whisky and headed back for it (it being cold, thirsty work walking across that field at night). I had collected a bottle and was just leaving the visitor centre area when I saw one of my mates coming toward me.

'Thinking on it later, I could even recall the man's stride. He was walking up from the graves area and, like me, was wrapped up against the cold in his kilt. I started to call to him but was distracted by something on the road. When I looked back to see who was coming to join me, he had gone. I stood for a while near the Well of the Dead and thought about this.

'I knew it was not a prank, or a joke, or someone out to scare me. We understood all too well the significance of this area and had agreed to move through it quickly and quietly on our way to the far end of the field. I really didn't know what to think. Off in the distance, our piper started to play and I walked out onto the open moor and headed for the sound. When I got to the group, it was clear no one had come back to meet me.

'Each of us said a few words as we looked around in the moonlight. Each man expressed his feelings of the time and place as best he could. We shared some whisky and our piper played. We made a pledge to each other, and to the site, to do our best in teaching and presenting the history that enveloped us.

'After a time, cold and jet lag began to pull at us. We were gathering ourselves up for the long walk back and had one last drink.

'There wasn't any discussion about what happened next. Each of us probably remembers it differently. I think that there, in the dark, someone tried to hand the bottle to someone who hadn't come in the van. Whatever happened, it was clear that the whisky was to stay and we were to go. The remaining half of the bottle we slowly poured out on the ground. It seems we were indeed intended to share *with* the spirits.'

❖ ❖ ❖

The significance of Culloden Field is brought home in each of these tales. In particular we can see its importance for people like the members of MacFarlanes' Company to whom we owe a debt due to their faithful recreation of the period.

Elliot promotes the portrayal of actual people and events from the rising, taking the view that 'the extensive research required to present real people benefits all of our events. Actual meetings and conversations are now able to be recreated. This approach has had a very positive impact on our work and continues to grow. Why do we do what we do? The mission of MacFarlanes' Company is to preserve, promote and present the history of peoples and their cultures. We believe that by understanding the past, you can better live in the present and better prepare for the future.'

## The Archaeologist's Tale

The Channel 4 TV unit arrived, back in 2001, disgorging a variety of different archaeological types in the general vicinity of the visitor centre. One of them in particular was going to be a frequent visitor over the next decade or more. This filming of *Two Men in a Trench* was only the beginning of a long and mutually beneficial relationship between Dr Tony Pollard and Culloden Battlefield.

By the time the Culloden Memorial Project was in full swing, Tony, working from Glasgow University, had excavated a reputation as one of the world's leading battlefield archaeologists. He has been back many times over the years, sometimes with extensive teams, sometimes with a leaner strike force. They use a variety of approaches, dependent upon what is deemed most appropriate, in the areas of the battlefield where they are active. I have seen them use a mix of geophysics, metal-detecting and trenching.

So what do they bring to light, in this earliest dawning of the twenty-first century? I am delighted to say that the major findings serve only to underline what we have always known about the battle.

However, new findings are always exciting and enlightening, and the archaeologists have had an excellent success rate at turning these up too and giving us the opportunity to reassess our thinking about some aspects of the battle. Overleaf is a map of the battlefield, which may clarify some of the findings that I will explore here.

Of particular interest within these pages are two quite remarkable discoveries, three significant and ongoing searches, and one very personal find. The find is a small oval pewter amulet (A) – a plaid brooch, being a Celtic cross. This would have belonged to a clansman and was found by Tony's team west of the Leanach enclosure, having been perhaps lost or torn from a Feileadh Mor in the midst of the action. It is highly poignant, as it brings the battle right down into close-range focus, and invests the conflict with an essential human reality, overstitched with the fragility of human belief.

The first of the big discoveries is the fact that the fiercest hand-to-hand fighting took place in the pastureland due south of the Well of the Dead (B).

The Highland regiments, which had, as usual, been placed in the front line, were the Jacobite shock troops. When the charge was ordered, these men surged down the field in huge combat wedges.

Previous theory had suggested that the Jacobite right wing (forced leftwards to avoid the Leanach stock enclosures) had crashed into the Jacobite centre, causing confusion even before the enemy were engaged in close combat. It was originally thought that the resulting mass of clansmen then hammered into the government front line by the Well of the Dead ... but this has now been disproved.

The archaeology, instead, provides clear evidence that the Jacobites charged straight towards the redcoats, undeflected by any enclosure walls, and that the heaviest fighting raged in the field some distance to the south of the Well of the Dead.

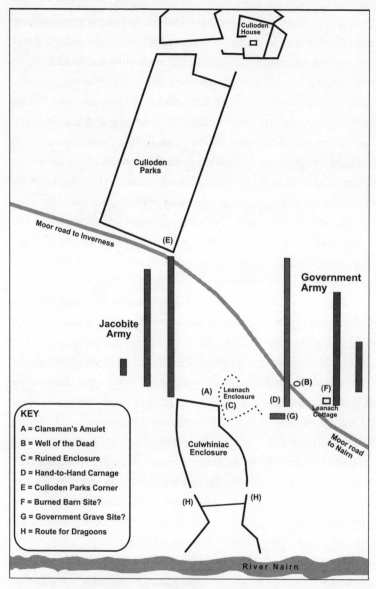

*Culloden battlefield, showing approximate pre-battle troop dispositions and marking eight points of further detail*

This could only have been possible if the Leanach enclosure was already a ruin in 1746 (C). It would be a sufficiently significant landscape feature to be included by contemporary military mappers, but perhaps only a course of stones high, thus causing no impediment to the onrushing troops. It can only be assumed that they loped easily across these degraded walls just moments before their ground-shaking impact with the government front lines.

This discovery that so much of the fighting took place in the big field south of the well is substantiated by the ground yielding up grapeshot distorted by having torn through individual Jacobites, just feet from leaving the cannon mouth. This, then, was the centre of the action (D), with Jacobites overwhelming some of the government artillery batteries, pushing back Barrell's and Munro's Regiments, but ultimately falling, many deep, on the right wing (in part due to the sustained enfilade fire from Wolfe's Regiment).

Another discovery with which archaeology sharpens our understanding of the battle is the use to which the government mortars were put. Cumberland had six Coehorn mortars under the command of Captain Lieutenant John Godwin. In the early part of the eighteenth century, mortars were only used in attacks on static targets, such as forts or houses, or to drop bombs over walls. These mortar shells looked like cartoon bombs – a big cannonball with a fuse in the top!

The American Revolutionary War was thought to be the first time that mortars were used against advancing enemy troops, but Tony Pollard has discovered differently. Mortar shell fragments have been found across the field at Culloden. This can only be because the Coehorn mortar crews in the government second line were continually raising their elevation in order to shorten the range, thereby keeping the Jacobites under fire as they raged across the field towards them.

Fragments of shell casings have also been found in the vicinity of the hand-to-hand fighting, indicating that the mortar bombs were still being hurled in, even after close combat had begun. The carnage would have been unbelievable and casualties from friendly fire would have been inevitable.

This use of mortars against an advancing enemy is currently the earliest known example of such anywhere, and adds another unique element to Culloden's military significance.

These discoveries will enhance the way that the story of Culloden is told in the future. But Tony is still looking for more. In particular, he is hunting for three specific locations.

The first of these is the corner of the Culloden Parks enclosure (E). This no longer exists above ground, but he is hopeful of finding it using geophysics. The payback for locating this position is that it will permit the exact location of the Jacobite front line to be charted. All of the maps and plans of the battle drawn at the time show the Jacobite line as anchored on the walls of the Culwhiniac enclosure to the south (a known point) and Culloden Parks to the north, at that point still to be found.

The second ongoing search is for evidence of the structure known as 'the Burned Barn'. The Reverend Robert Forbes describes it in *The Lyon in Mourning* thus:

> At a small distance from the field there was a hut for sheltering sheep and goats in stormy weather. To this hut some of the wounded men had crawled, but were soon found out by the soldiery, who made sure the door, and set fire to several parts of the hut, so that all within it perished in the flames, to the number of between thirty and forty persons, among whom were some beggars, who had been spectators of the battle, in hopes of sharing in the plunder. Many people went and viewed the smothered and scorched bodies among the rubbish of the hut. Sure the poor beggars could not be deemed rebels in any sense whatsoever.

It has long been rumoured that this barn was part of the collection of buildings at Leanach Cottage. However, despite repeated trenching, the archaeologists have found not a trace of a charcoal layer in the soil. Given the lack of any firm evidence as to such a building's whereabouts, they are starting to wonder if it might even lie under the existing visitor centre (F).

If that is indeed the case, then people will not have too long to wait to find out for sure. The clock is ticking on the existing centre; once the new centre is up and running, the old one will be demolished (I have seen more than one trowel twitching in anticipation of access).

The third and final search that I will refer to here concerns the last resting place for the government dead killed during the battle. The story of Culloden will be told in greater detail once the new centre opens, due in part to the growing body of knowledge available to us but also because the National Trust for Scotland has acquired more of the battlefield and its surrounds, allowing more of the action to be illustrated where it happened. Part of this interpretation will include new paths.

As a mark of respect to the fallen, we need to find the government grave, thus ensuring that no such paths are constructed over it.

It is worth noting, too, that the area of the historical burial site is mistakenly called the Field of the English. The irony here is that the highest mortality rates on the government side were suffered by Barrell's and Munro's Regiments, both of which recruited heavily in the Scottish Lowlands, so the field in question could just as easily be referred to as the 'Field of the Lowland Scot'.

After some sustained input, using geophysics to map a large portion of the field, two possible locations for this grave were found. Then, in early April 2005, during the metal-detector phase, a very significant find was made at the second of these two locations, 60 yards south-east of the Well of the Dead. One of the archaeologists found a silver coin of reasonably high face value. This was one of those small finds with a big possibility attached.

It was a German coin, a 12 Thaler piece, dated 1752. Tony is convinced that it represents the jackpot in relation to his search for the government grave (G). As it post-dates the battle, he is fairly sure that it was probably lost, or left, by a trooper (possibly even stationed at Fort George after 1757) who had been making a visit to the grave of fallen former comrades-in-arms.

This is a persuasive argument and makes a powerful counter-balance at human level to the clansman's amulet which began this tale. It also represents Culloden as a site of pilgrimage, and a heritage icon, from those early visits through the present time and into the future.

# Epilogue

Culloden – an emotive word and an emotive place. A place rich in stories, of which those included within these pages are but a small portion. The stories have been used, in most cases, to highlight different facts about the battle and also to dispense with some common misconceptions. This epilogue gives a further opportunity to revisit the facts as outlined earlier:

- This battle was not Scotland against England. It was a British civil war between the Houses of Stuart and Hanover
- The principal religious difference on the field was not Catholic versus Protestant; it was Protestant Presbyterian versus Protestant Episcopalian
- The Jacobite army was neither a clan army nor a Highland army. Highlanders made up only about 45 per cent of the army's total fighting strength
- There were large numbers of Lowland Scots serving with the Jacobite forces
- Although little mercy was shown to many of the Jacobite wounded on the field of Culloden, many prisoners *were* taken: altogether, throughout the '45 rising, the prisoners numbered almost 3,500 in total
- There were many more Scots fighting with Prince Charlie than were fighting against him. Even the Cumberland Papers state that the redcoat forces included only some 2,284 Scots

These tales, presented here for you, are mainly – but not entirely – told from a Jacobite perspective. This is understandable and to be expected.

The House of Hanover was the victorious dynasty on the field of Culloden. It is often said that the victors of armed struggle write the history thereafter. That much is true, and more is true besides. The victors remake society through cultures and institutions comfortable to them. We therefore inhabit a society and economy that is a legacy of the House of Hanover. One aspect of such a world was the sustained attempt to remove any vestige of Highland culture, irrespective of the fact that many of the clans had been loyal to George II and had fought for him in the '45 rising.

This is why balance is a difficult concept in regard to Culloden. The outcome of the battle was not balanced, and neither was the political and military aftermath, so the place means different things to different people.

The descendants of the supporters of the House of Stuart are by far the most frequent visitors to the moor. For them, a trip to the site is like a heritage pilgrimage; the battlefield is an icon. The history of the defeated becomes the hidden history, often as secrets that are held in the oral tradition and passed with care and accuracy from generation to generation.

The last stand of a lost cause becomes the place around which tales and stories gather. Some of these are little more than tattered strips of mist, bits of myth and legend. Others, however, are like the Jacobite standards themselves, rescued from the field, real and precious, and held in trust for posterity.

Taken together, these tales shape our perception of the Culloden of today and are a powerful and significant part of the heritage culture of many countries around the world.

# Whistling

By its very nature, Culloden is an emotive place to work. The horror and tragedy that unfolded on the field is affecting for staff as well as visitors. We see at least one or two people a month overcome and in tears, saying that the sadness and the sense of loss are palpable. So, a little like whistling past the graveyard gates, we sometimes use a little humour to keep our spirits up.

The following are some of the more unusual comments received at the ticket desk, the visitors being from a mix of places, including Britain, Australia and the USA:

- I've paid £5, but I can't find your castle anywhere!
- This is the most beautiful part of Ireland we've been to so far!
- Is this where the battle was, son?
  Yes indeed!
  Gee, it's an awfully small building. How did they get all the men in here?
- Do I need to be punched, or stamped on, to go to the ladies' room? (This lady was referring to her ticket.)
- Do I *have* to go outside to visit the battlefield?
- Is this the battle that Mel Gibson fought in?
- Where do I get the boat for my Loch Lomond experience? (I was asked this after the visitors had followed their TomTom navigator to entirely the wrong Balloch, some three and a half hours too far north!)

- Do we *have* to go to the movie?
- 'Bonnie' should have spoken to me before the battle!
- Which end of the field did the confederates stand at? (Not as daft a question as it at first sounds, given the identification that the American South has with the Jacobite cause.)
- I'm not interested in battlefields; aren't you the Moors Peat Centre?

So, thank you to the authors of the above statements for lightening the mood. Here's hoping for more than a few more over forthcoming years.

# Select Bibliography

Anderson, Peter, *Culloden Moor and the Story of the Battle*, 1867

Bain, George, *History of Nairnshire*, 'Telegraph' Office, Nairn, 1928

Bain, George, *The Lordship of Petty*, 'Telegraph' Office, Nairn, 1925

Barclay, Gordon, *Farmers, Temples and Tombs: Scotland in the Neolithic and Early Bronze Age*, Birlinn Ltd, Edinburgh, 2005

Berry, C. Leo, *The Young Pretender's Mistress*, Charles Skilton Ltd, Edinburgh, 1977

Blaikie, Walter Biggar, *Itinerary of Prince Charles Edward Stuart*, Scottish History Society, 1897

Bradley, Richard, *The Good Stones: A New Investigation of the Clava Cairns*, Society of Antiquaries of Scotland, 2000

Bruce, George, and Paul H. Scott (eds), *A Scottish Postbag: Eight Centuries of Scottish Letters*, The Saltire Society, Edinburgh, 2002

*Clan Chattan* (Journal of the Clan Chattan Association), Vol. IX, No. 5, 1993

Craig, Maggie, *Damn' Rebel Bitches: The Women of the '45*, Mainstream Publishing, Edinburgh, 2000

Dickinson, William Croft, *Scotland from the Earliest Times to 1603*, Oxford University Press, Oxford, 1977

Dodgshon, Robert, *The Age of the Clans: The Highlands from Somerled to the Clearances*, Birlinn Ltd, Edinburgh, 2002

Donaldson, Professor Gordon (ed.), *Scottish Historical Documents*, Neil Wilson Publishing, Glasgow, 1997

Douglas, Hugh, *Flora MacDonald: The Most Loyal Rebel*, Sutton Publishing Ltd, Stroud, 2003

Duffy, Christopher, *The '45*, Cassell, London, 2003

Dunlop, Jean, *The Clan Chisholm*, Johnston and Bacon Ltd, Edinburgh, 1953

Forbes, Revd Robert, *The Lyon in Mourning*, Scottish Academic Press, Edinburgh, 1975

Fraser-Mackintosh, Charles, *An Account of the Confederation of Clan Chattan*, published by John Mackay, *Celtic Monthly*, Glasgow, 1898

Gibson, John Sibbald, *Lochiel of the '45: The Jacobite Chief and the Prince*, Edinburgh University Press Ltd, Edinburgh, 1994

Grant, I.F., *The Clan Grant*, Johnston and Bacon Ltd, Edinburgh, 1955

Hadden, J. Cuthbert, *Prince Charles Edward*, Sir Isaac Pitman & Sons, London, 1913

Hunter, James, *Culloden, and the Last Clansman*, Mainstream Publishing, Edinburgh, 1994

Johnstone, James Chevalier de, *Memoirs of the Rebellion in 1745 and 1746*, London, 1822

Lenman, Bruce, *The Jacobite Clans of the Great Glen 1650–1784*, Scottish Cultural Press, Dalkeith, 2004

Linklater, Eric, *The Prince in the Heather*, Granada Publishing Ltd, Herts, 1976

Livingstone, Alastair, Christian Aikman and Betty S. Hart (eds), *No Quarter Given: The Muster Roll of Prince Charles Edward Stuart's Army, 1745–46*, Neil Wilson Publishing, Glasgow, 2001

Lord Elcho, *The Affairs of Scotland 1744–1746*, David Douglas, Edinburgh, 1907

MacDonald, Charles, *Moidart: Among the Clanranalds*, Birlinn, Edinburgh, 1997

Macdonald, Donald J., *Clan Donald*, Macdonald Publishers, Loanhead, 1978

MacDonald, Norman H., *The Clan Ranald of Lochaber*, no publisher quoted

MacKay, Dr James, *Pocket History of Scotland*, Lomond Books, 2003

Mackenzie, Alexander, *History of the Chisholms*, the "Scottish Highlander" office, 1891

McKerral, Andrew, *The Clan Campbell*, Johnston and Bacon Ltd, Edinburgh, 1953

Mackintosh of Mackintosh, Margaret, *The History of the Clan Mackintosh and the Clan Chattan*, Macdonald Publishers, Midlothian, 1982

Maxwell, Gordon, *A Gathering of Eagles: Scenes from Roman Scotland*, Birlinn Ltd, Edinburgh, 2005

Miller, James, *Inverness: A History*, Birlinn Ltd, Edinburgh, 2004

Mills, Hazel, *Scottish Quotations*, HarperCollins Publishers, Glasgow, 1999

Moffat, William, *A History of Scotland*, Vols 1, 2 and 3, Oxford University Press, 1985

Murray, C. de B., *Duncan Forbes of Culloden*, International Publishing Company, London, 1936

Pittock, Murray G.H., *The Myth of the Jacobite Clans*, Edinburgh University Press, 1995

Prebble, John, *Culloden*, Pimlico, London, 2002

Reid, Stuart, *Culloden 1746: Battlefield Guide*, Pen and Sword Books Ltd, South Yorkshire, 2005

Seton, Sir Bruce, and Jean Arnot, *Prisoners of the '45*, edited from the State Papers, The Scottish History Society, 1928

Simpson, Peter A., *Culloden and the Four Unjust Men*, Peter A. Simpson, 2000

Szechi, Daniel, *The Jacobites, Britain & Europe 1688–1788*, Manchester University Press, 1994

Tacitus, *The Agricola and the Germania*, Penguin Books, Middlesex, 1970

*The Appin Mystery*, West Highlands & Islands of Argyll Tourist Board Ltd, 1992

Tomasson, Katherine, and Francis Buist, *Battles of the '45*, Pan Books, London, 1967

Tranter, Nigel, *The North East: The Shires of Banff, Moray, Nairn, with Easter Inverness and Easter Ross*, Hodder and Stoughton, London, 1974

Wemyss, Alice, *Elcho of the '45*, The Saltire Society, Edinburgh, 2003

Youngson, A.J., *The Prince and the Pretender: Two Views of the '45*, Mercat Press, Edinburgh, 1996

A broad range of contemporary newspapers, manuscript sources, and documentary collections were accessed at the National Library of Scotland, Inverness Library, the National Trust for Scotland Library, the National Archives of Scotland and the National Archives at Kew.

# INDEX